GOSPEL MEMORIES

The Future Can Rewrite Our Past

Jake Owensby

Morehouse Publishing
NEW YORK

Unless otherwise noted, the Scripture quotations contained herein are from the New Revised Standard Version Bible, copyright © 1989 by the Division of Christian Education of the National Council of Churches of Christ in the U.S.A. Used by permission. All rights reserved.

Morehouse Publishing, 19 East 34th Street, New York, NY 10016

Morehouse Publishing is an imprint of Church Publishing Incorporated.

www.churchpublishing.org

Cover design by Laurie Klein Westhafer
Typeset by Denise Hoff

Library of Congress Cataloging-in-Publication Data

Owensby, Jake.
    Gospel memories : the future can rewrite our past / Jake Owensby.
      pages cm
    Includes bibliographical references and index.
      ISBN 978-0-8192-3265-6 (pbk.)—ISBN 978-0-8192-3266-3 (ebook)
  1. Owensby, Jake.   2. Episcopal Church—Louisiana—Bishops—Biography.
  3. Christian biography—Louisiana.   I. Title.
BX5995.O94A3 2016
283.092—dc23
[B]   2015029132

Printed in the United States of America

To Trudy,
Joseph, and
Marie...
Bis morgen!

Contents

Part Four: Film, Fiction, Life

Part Five: Growing Up, Sort of

Acknowledgments

To Charlene Klister and Margaret Houck: Thank you for believing in me and encouraging me early and often.

To Rudi Makkreel, Tom Flynn, and Kent Linville: Thank you for pushing me to be clear and to seek the truth.

To my spiritual friends Dennis Campbell, Charles DuBois, and Nathaniel Pyron: You listened as I told, revised, and retold the stories of my life and sought God's presence in it. You gently and patiently nudged me each time to deeper honesty. I am grateful for your wisdom, grace, and friendship.

To Susan Goff, Nick Knisely, and Jeff Fisher, my bishop friends and classmates: You took time from ridiculously busy schedules to read, to respond, and to offer support. Thank you!

To my editor Sharon Ely Pearson: Our conversations motivated me and helped me to rethink and reshape this book. You shared your talent and enthusiasm with me by the truckload. I am truly grateful for your expertise and your friendship. Additional thanks go to Ryan Masteller and Sandra Chiles for expertly guiding and improving my manuscript through production.

To the people of the Episcopal Diocese of Western Louisiana: Thank you for letting me try out and revise and revise again the thoughts that coalesced into this book. Your listening ears and your thoughtful responses to sermons, classes, and conversations were a wonderful gift. I look forward to being creative together for years to come.

To my diocesan staff Kathy Richey, Holly Davis, Joy Owensby, Ron Clingenpeel, Bill Bryant, Bette Kaufmann, Mitzi

George, and Liz Ratcliffe: Thank you for being so good at what you do that I have the gift of time to write.

And finally, to my wife, Joy, my daughter, Meredith, and my sons, Andrew and Patrick: Thank you for putting up with me, for making me laugh, and for teaching me the really important stuff in life.

Introduction

I'm about midway through my fourth year as a bishop in the Episcopal Church. I've been on a steep learning curve. But the curve I'm on is probably not the one you've got in mind.

Oh sure, my job in the Church has changed in countless ways. Only bishops confirm and ordain, and we wear miters and carry crosiers. Our administrative responsibilities differ significantly from those of parish priests. Every Sunday I'm in a different congregation, so I don't know where anything is or how anything works.

All of this is the usual stuff of being a new bishop. But there's something more. Maybe it's my new role in the Church or my place in the life cycle or the result of moving to a new, more rural part of Louisiana. Whatever the reason, I've been reflecting on old memories. Seeing events in my life from a different angle. Weaving them anew into the story I tell of my life.

The lens through which I've been seeing my life is the Gospel. I want to be clear about this. Sometimes I've used events in my life to illustrate the Gospel. Precisely the opposite has been going on for the last few years. Meditating on the Gospel narratives is actively reshaping not only my memories but transforming my past.

Now that must sound odd. The past is the past. Right? It's water under the bridge. In both counseling and spiritual direction, reflecting upon my past has helped to illuminate who I've become today. But I've found that the Gospel's power is working in me in the opposite direction. The future is rewriting my past.

Please don't get me wrong. The brute facts of my past remain the same. I was born in 1957. My mother, Trudy, emigrated from Austria following the Second World War, having survived the Nazi concentration camp Mauthausen. She and my abusive father, Sam, divorced when I was ten. I really was born with a cleft palate that went uncorrected until adulthood. And as improbable as it is, this blue-collar kid from an ill-educated family earned a PhD in philosophy and eventually became a bishop in the Episcopal Church.

You see, many of us assume that our past shapes our future. And there is a kind of truth to this. But the Gospel is all about the counterintuitive promise that God is shaping us right now toward the divine vision of who we will become. It is not our past that makes us into the image of God. God's redeeming love does that. In God, who we are not yet is shaping who we become.

And as I stumble and scooch and sidestep my way toward resembling this true self, the meaning of the twists and turns of my past changes. Some of the bruises and the wounds I once resented and would just as soon have forgotten have taken on a different hue. They don't make me what I am today. What I am today makes them, through the power of the Gospel, the soil from which wider life is emerging.

God is transforming my past into a fabric of Gospel memories. The future keeps changing the meaning of my past. There's more than a lot of healing going on in me as a result. I can't be sure, but I think that maybe, just maybe, that's how God works with lots of us. That is why I offer you the pages that follow.

In the chapters that follow I share events, films, and pieces of literature as my Gospel memories. This is not meant to be a memoir, even though it contains autobiographical elements. My hope is that as I share my Gospel memories with you, you will experience Gospel memories of your own. My hope is that you will experience the joy, the surprise, and the healing of God's future rewriting your past.

To facilitate this process, each chapter provides a reference to a Gospel story. While you may read each chapter without reference to the biblical text, spending time reflecting on scripture may enhance your experience. Similarly, each chapter ends with some reflection questions. They are an invitation to deeper engagement. The questions can serve both personal reflection and group conversation.

Whether you use this book as a personal devotional or share it as a catalyst for small group interaction, my hope is that it will in some way aid you in the shaping of your own Gospel memories.

PART ONE

Speaking Plainly

Raise your words, not your voice.
It is rain that grows flowers, not thunder.

Rumi

1

Is God Fair?

Read John 11:1–45

It's not fair. Life, that is. Life is not fair.

So, where is God in that?

I've had some occasions to think just those thoughts. Maybe you have, too. One of those occasions came when I was just a child.

I was the new kid in the first-grade class at Louisville Academy, just starting to feel like I might actually fit in. Louisville sits in the midst of southern Georgia farmland. Fewer than two thousand people live there.

Not many people move into Louisville. The residents are not practiced at making strangers feel at home. Add to the towns-folk's wariness toward strangers that I was burdened with a profound speech impediment, and you'll understand why I struggled to belong.

One day we had a substitute teacher. The only thing that I remember from that class session is an art activity. I traced a squirrel and then colored in the picture. All of us crowded around to tell the substitute about our drawing.

With all my classmates peering over my shoulder, the teacher asked me, "What is that?"

"A squirrel," I said.

"What?"

"A squirrel."

"Go sit down and come back when you learn to talk."

I can still feel the blood rush to my face and the eyes of all my classmates staring at me. Lacking a soft palate, I was physically incapable of making the "s" sound. All the breath passed through my nose, and a sound emerged something like "Hwhwquirl." The teacher's words reminded me (and announced to my classmates) that where I came from and how I was made meant that I did not belong.

Life is not fair.

Where was God when I was born with a cleft palate, when my parents couldn't afford to get it fixed, when that church-going lady told a deformed, vulnerable little boy to sit down and shut up because she couldn't understand his distorted speech?

If you insist that God can be God only by preventing suffering and heartache, injustice and oppression, cruelty and indifference, then you are going to have a very difficult time finding God in this world.

But as it turns out, God does the very best work in the midst of the worst that this world throws at us. That's one of the lessons we learn from the story of Jesus raising Lazarus from the dead.

Jesus arrives in Bethany after Lazarus has been dead and buried for four days. Lazarus's sisters, Mary and Martha, had sent for him while Lazarus was ill, but Jesus delayed in coming.

Martha and Mary each greet Jesus with the same words. "Lord, if you had been here, my brother would not have died."[1]

Maybe they simply meant, "If only you could have gotten here sooner, you could have healed Lazarus."

---

1 John 11:21, 32.

Or maybe they were more accusatory in their grief: "What kept you? You should have been here. You could have have saved him!"

In any event, Mary and Martha looked to Jesus to prevent a heartrending catastrophe. This is perfectly understandable. Mary and Martha loved their brother. As his health declined and his life seemed to be slipping away, they turned to God for help.

Like them, and like many of us, I've done precisely the same thing. I pray for a long list of people every day, many of whom are suffering from an intractable disease, facing surgery, or undergoing treatment.

I believe that God loves us and that God's love is more than just an emotion. It's a practice, a habitual way of acting toward the ones God loves. To say that God loves us, to say that God loves me, is to say that God wants the very best for me and is working actively to bring that good about all the time.

Some of us experience suffering and untimely death, disappointment, and hardship as a betrayal by God. For instance, in my prior life as a philosophy professor I had a student in one of my classes who grew angry and verbally abusive. We were discussing how to reconcile our concept of a good God with suffering in the world. When I asked him where his anger was coming from, he initially told me that he is a bishop's son. (Well, that explained a lot.) Then he told me that his best friend had died in a car crash. His friend had suffered terribly before succumbing to his injuries.

My student said, "He didn't have to die. God didn't have to let him die. And even if he did, God didn't have to let him die like that. If God was really all that good he could have let him just go to sleep. To drift on up to heaven without all that blood and pain."

Life is not fair.

And if God's love for us means that God will prevent bad things from happening to us and to the ones we love, then let's face it. We can't say that God loves us.

The story of Lazarus gives us a different perspective on God's love for us. Sometimes God does prevent suffering. Sometimes God relieves suffering. But most fundamentally, God's love transforms suffering and even death. If we look for God merely to prevent suffering in our lives, we're expecting entirely too little from God.

Jesus wept at Lazarus's tomb. God does not stand at a safe distance from the changes and the chances, the emotional bruises, and the physical misery of this life. In Jesus, God jumps in with both feet.

While God's presence is comforting, Jesus enters our life to do more than go down with us on our sinking ship. Alternatively, we may expect Jesus to wave a magic wand and make it all go away. But that's not how it works either.

Jesus transforms our suffering, our sorrow, and even our death from the inside out. From heartbreak, Jesus creates a compassionate heart. From suffering, Jesus inspires hands that heal. And most crucially—definitive of who God is and what God is making of our lives—from death itself God brings a new kind of life. A life that has passed through suffering and death by the power of God. A life that is forever beyond want, agony, shame, loneliness, and death itself.

God is about more than comfort, safety, entertainment, and fun. God is about resurrection. Endless, boundless joy, tranquility, and belonging. God imparts a new kind of life in Jesus. And God is doing that already. Right now. Our relationship with God is transforming us.

Jesus delayed in coming to Bethany precisely because he loved Lazarus, Mary, and Martha. Preventing Lazarus's death would have been only a temporary measure. After all, he would have died eventually in any event. God wants more for Lazarus than a few extra years. He wants eternal life. And he wants it right now, not just after Lazarus's biological life is over.

Jesus stood before the tomb and called Lazarus out of death into life. It is true that Lazarus would die again. But by raising Lazarus from the dead, Jesus showed everybody present that day—he shows you and me—that he is already imparting the eternal life that we will inhabit fully some day. Jesus is gradually speaking new life, a new kind of life, into his friends.

As we grow into this new life, we are drawn into God's mission of bringing new life from suffering and death. Remember, when Lazarus stumbles from the tomb, he is wrapped in death clothes from head to toe. Jesus tells his followers to unbind him.

Jesus gives new life. But this new life takes some getting used to. We need help from those around us. Somebody has to help us get rid of old death clothes that no longer suit us. And we can do that for others.

Whether those clothes are emotional habits, like old resentments and bitterness, or the social injustices, like payday loans and unjust wages, Jesus sends you and me into the world to unbind the friends he has already called from the tomb.

Let us return to that first-grade episode for just a moment. I returned to my seat lonely and aching. Little could I have known that God was already working in me what I could not do for myself.

Instead of letting me shrink into a tomb of my own making, God stirred up some courage in me that I cannot account for. I actually started speaking up more in class and on the playground. Being told to shut up, I discovered that I had something to say.

God instilled a love of writing in me. And the Holy One placed people in my life who nurtured that love and sharpened my skills. Sister Charlene Klister and Dr. Margaret McKenna Houck in high school. Professors Kent Linville, Hoyt Oliver, Rudi Makkreel, and Tom Flynn. Each in their own way encouraged and pushed me to say what I had to say with my pen (and eventually my laptop).

And then one day, Dr. Hutson Carspecken corrected my cleft palate. I could say with my lips what I had learned to say with the written word. And people could understand me.

Life is not fair. And fair is not good enough for God.

God wants for us more than a life anesthetized by comfort and decorated with material possessions, more than a life measured by our fleeting achievements, our moral rectitude, and our presumed spiritual superiority.

God wants for us a life transformed by the divine presence in its very midst. A life that is overflowing with God's love. And that is just what God is doing through Christ.

Reflection Questions

- Imagine that you are Mary or Martha. You have sent for Jesus to heal your brother Lazarus, but he doesn't come. Lazarus dies. What are you feeling and thinking about Jesus?
- Tell a story about a difficult time in your life when you struggled to see God at work or couldn't see God at all. Be as specific as you can. What were you feeling and thinking about God?
- If you still cannot see how God responded to that situation, how is that shaping your relationship with God now? What do you want to say to God about that?
- If, on looking back, you can see how God was at work, what did that teach you about your true self? About God?

2

Christmas Lights, a Junkyard, and the Manger

Read Luke 2:8–14

My eyelids sprang open at three in the morning. Christmas morning. I was seven years old. My half brother Joel—already twelve and too cool for kid stuff—lay sleeping soundly next to me on a makeshift cot in the dining room.

Fueled by the anticipation of Santa's arrival and a record-shattering blood sugar level, my whole body had been vibrating with excitement all night. Around nine o'clock my parents had turned out all the lights in a vain attempt to get me to sleep. In the pitch dark I lay, counting the minutes impatiently, until sometime around midnight the sugar bender I was on finally came to a crashing halt.

But now I was fully alert. A glow seeped out of the living room behind us and poured itself thinly across the dining room floor. A faint, warm light coaxed recognizable shapes out of the darkness: the dining room table, the window frame, the doorway leading out toward the kitchen.

"Santa's come," I whispered to Joel.

No response.

I shook his shoulder and said directly in his ear, "Santa's come."

"Go back to sleep," he said. "It's three o'clock in the morning. You can't wake them up this early."

"But Santa's come! He turned on the Christmas tree lights."

This was back in the day before LED lights. Christmas tree bulbs burned hot, so you had to turn off the lights at night for fear of the tree catching fire and the house burning down. If the lights were on, I knew that only Santa could have turned them on to let us know that he had been there.

"Alright," said Joel. "Look, you can't wake them up. But I'll let you tiptoe to the door and peek in. Then you have to get back in bed and wait until at least five o'clock."

I slipped out from under the covers and crept to the living room doorway. Stepping across the threshold, I caught my breath. The gold foil wrapping the gifts captured the tree's light and then cast it into the air like glimmering fairy dust.

Now you might think that I was excited about the gifts. But that wasn't it. I was transfixed by the light and by what that light was doing to the room. I couldn't have told you at the time. But it wasn't just the light that took my breath away. It was what the light conveyed. It announced a presence, a presence that was transforming everything from the inside out.

For just a moment, I stood in a place whose very air smelled of welcome. If you have ever felt another's delight in you, then you know what the golden light was whispering wordlessly to my soul. The energy that brought all things to be and holds all things together was murmuring in the innermost chambers of my heart: "You are my child. You are enough."

I had sat in that room thousands of times, and yet I was transported to a place that I had only dimly hoped might exist. A place where I was completely okay and all was well. A place where meanness and pettiness never marred beauty. A place where trust was never violated. A place with no fear of rejection or want or loss.

The contrast with what anyone else would have seen and heard at my old address would have been jarring.

We lived in a shabby two-bedroom, one-bath house. It could not have been much bigger than eight hundred square feet. The weathered wood of the front porch sorely needed painting and routinely shed splinters into my bare feet.

The yard was a patchwork of weeds and dirt. The driveway was a two-track dirt path, beaten by the repeated wear of car tires leading to a tumbledown shed out back.

To one side of the house lay an independent gas station and mechanic shop. It wasn't much more than a pole barn with a garage. The smell of old oil and grease sat like a cloud over the place.

Behind the house stretched a junkyard littered with old car and truck bodies. Packards and Studebakers, ancient pickups and smashed station wagons lay scattered haphazardly around the lot. Many had hoods up and doors open, having been scavenged for cheap spare parts by clever do-it-yourself mechanics.

Inside our cramped and battered house the air was thick with discord. My father was controlling and abusive. My mother was beaten and wary but unbroken. Their marriage was dissolving, and a hole in the universe was opening just beneath my feet.

Joel did not live with us much of the time. Mostly, he lived with his own mother, sister, and another half-brother by his stepfather. But when he was with us, his persistent resentment toward me for being part of that other family came in the form of punches to the belly and jokes poked at my flabby clumsiness.

So you see, it is quite remarkable that something that I can only call holy infiltrated that drab and messy space with an uncanny joy and an inexplicable peace. On that night, a cluttered, dingy living room was infused with the Kingdom of God.

When I let myself slow down, I still feel that light on my face and see it shimmering between young lovers and old couples, on frazzled parents and squirmy children, around homeless veterans and crabby checkout clerks.

It shines to this day in common, unlikely, and even scandalous places. That's why I've come to believe that the Christmas light that enthralled me so many years ago was the same light that illuminated the night sky above a scruffy group of shepherds on the outskirts of Bethlehem.

And as those shepherds drew near to a stable in a back alley in the shabbiest part of a crummy little town, that same light dusted the dirt floor, the straw, and the livestock of a ramshackle manger with that same warm, gentle glow.

In Jesus, God was—God is—infusing the earth with the very light of heaven.

This earth. In all its danger and its comfort, its violence and its tenderness, its chaos and its beauty, its heartbreak and its promise.

This earth. Where wars rage, gangs clash over turf, and children go to bed hungry.

This earth. Where streets are filled with protests and parades. Where old prejudices persist and addicts get sober.

This earth. Where mothers hold new babies, children take their first steps, and families gather to share their deep and ragged love for each other.

The light of heaven that bathed me that night did not flicker and go out. It is neither intermittent nor inconsistent. It is gently persistent, gradually scattering itself into all of earth's dark corners.

Christ was born in Bethlehem to bring the very light of heaven to earth. Not just once. But once and for all. That light will never be extinguished, because in Jesus its very source—God—has come to dwell in our midst.

Reflection Questions

- Imagine that you are one of the shepherds on the outskirts of Bethlehem. God's presence becomes so real to you that it seems to make everything glow from the inside out. And God is speaking to you. Personally. What is God saying?

- Tell a story about a time when God seemed very present to you in an unlikely place or in a very common place. How would you describe God's presence? What message did God bring to you in that encounter?

- If you have never had an experience like this, talk about what it is like to hear someone else relate their own story. Do you feel skeptical? Do you wish to have such an encounter yourself? Would you rather not? What do you make of such stories?

- What do you want to hear God say to you today?

3

Spiritual Spanx

Read Matthew 22:1–14

During my early childhood my family did not attend worship services. My father was Baptist and my mother was Roman Catholic. Their spiritual differences partly explain our Sunday absence from the pews.

My introduction to the Roman Catholic Mass came when I was in fourth grade. Eventually I was baptized in the Roman Church and attended Catholic schools. But my early lack of a faith community did not deter my mother from buying Sunday clothes for me.

In the autumn of my third-grade year my mother bought me a tan, three-piece corduroy suit. We had traveled forty miles from little Louisville to what seemed like the big city of Augusta. At Belk's, my mother put the suit on layaway and paid for it over time. We picked it up after the final payment sometime around Thanksgiving.

That suit hung in my closet until the last day before Christmas break. Since we were having a party in our third-grade class, my Old World mother encouraged me to wear the suit. I was sort of reluctant. Austrian kids might have dressed up for school parties, but the kids from rural Louisville were going to show up with blue jean legs rolled up so as not to drag the floor and brogan boots. In other words, everybody else would be wearing what I normally wore.

Not wanting to disappoint my mom, I wore the suit. If you've ever worn a corduroy anything, you know that the fabric is stiff when it's new. You have to wear it quite a bit to break it in. A whole suit made of corduroy felt like a suit of medieval armor. I couldn't properly bend my arms or my legs, so I walked sort of like the Tin Man from the Wizard of Oz seriously in need of his oil can.

These days, a lot of clothes and shoes come ready to wear. There's no breaking in period, or at least not one you really notice. But some things are still like that corduroy suit. They take some breaking in. Before its repeated wearing has molded your jacket or pair of shoes to the contours of your body, they pinch, bind, and restrict your natural movements. Eventually, though, apparel folds and bends along with you. It's like your second skin.

Now I ask you to use your imagination to invert this process. Picture a suit of clothes that, instead of conforming to the body and its habitual motions, molds your body. Something like Spanx. Only, over time these garments begin to lend a permanent new shape to your body. Muffin tops gradually give way to youthful curves. Beer bellies become chiseled abs.

That would be quite a product! It would fly off the shelves. At least, that's what would happen initially. The first customers would soon discover that these garments are uncomfortable. They squeeze and press, cut off the circulation, and make it hard to breathe. Being shaped by something beyond yourself takes time and will probably involve being stretched and cramped in turn.

Following Jesus involves just that: submitting to being stretched by something—by someone—beyond ourselves.

Jesus shapes our hearts and minds. Some seem to think that this is solely an inside-out job. Jesus changes our hearts and minds, and then Christlike behavior follows as a result. But strictly speaking, Christ changes us from the inside out and from the outside in.

Sometimes Jesus initially touches our hearts and our minds from the inside. But even in such cases, the heart and the mind have a long way to go. Jesus continues his shaping and stretching work from the outside in. When Jesus issues the Great Commission—make disciples of all nations—he is sending his followers on an outside-in job. Many of us have assumed that the Great Commission instructs us to change hearts and minds so that changed lives will result. A closer look at Jesus' teaching suggests that he wants us to change lives. Hearts and minds will follow.

You might say that Jesus offers us Spiritual Spanx. The Way of Christ is a new way of living. A way that Jesus has patterned for us. Initially, it will seem like an ill-fitting suit of clothes. The life that Jesus patterns for us will cramp and stretch us in turn. Just think back to your own childhood. How did that sharing thing go for you at first? Or, if you are in recovery, remember those first few months of groping for and struggling toward sobriety. Did your sponsor ever say to just suit up and show up? And yet, over time, acting like Jesus will help us increasingly to think, feel, and desire just like Jesus.

That's one of the lessons Jesus conveys when he relates the familiar parable of the wedding feast.

A king throws a regular wingding for his son. He invites all his friends and associates. None of them come. They're too busy, have a better offer, or just don't care. Eventually, the king fills the dining hall with people dragged off the streets: strangers, slackers, lowlifes, wallflowers, street artists, dog walkers, mimes, and meter maids. Anybody his servants can grab.

So far so good. Everything Jesus says fits nicely with our view of the God of Grace. The Holy One invites all comers because of who God is, not because of who we are.

But the parable starts to turn dark—and to challenge our contemporary sensibilities—when the king stumbles upon an inappropriately dressed guest. Apparently, attendance at this banquet requires a customary wedding garment. This particular guest seems still to be wearing his street clothes.

You might reasonably wonder how someone who was just dragged off the street might be expected to be wearing the formal attire that the king demands. After all, mere moments before the start of the festivities, the person was writing a parking ticket or annoying sidewalk diners with a mime performance. Most of us don't carry around a tuxedo or an evening gown on the off chance that a complete stranger will suddenly drag us into a formal dinner party.

Let's sweep this concern aside by admitting up front that Jesus is not especially concerned with historical accuracy or even dramatic coherence here. He's trying to make a theological point, not write a newspaper account or a short story. This is a parable.

And here's the point: God's grace originates with God. We don't earn it. But neither should we presume upon it. Genuinely accepting God's invitation to be in relationship means submitting ourselves to being transformed by the love that God offers. In other words, accepting the invitation involves putting on "Spiritual Spanx": acting like Christ on the outside before we resemble Christ fully on the inside.

Spiritual Spanx will pinch and bind each of us in different ways. Each person is born with spiritual strengths and spiritual challenges. God's molding and shaping is always highly personalized.

Perseverance comes naturally to some. When they don't get that first job or the first test grade is bad or the initial trip to the gym feels like medieval torture, these folks are energized. Knock them down and they pop up feeling an increased sense of determination.

Others initially feel discouraged by adversity and setbacks. They fear that things won't work out. Nevertheless, they fight through that fear to seek that next job, to find a new study strategy for the next test, and to get back into the gym. Adversity and setbacks teach them the perseverance they lack.

Similarly, some people are constitutionally patient. They would never dream of finishing your sentences, fuming in traffic behind a slow driver, or shouting at a child for spilling milk. By contrast, some have to bite their lip to let someone else complete her thought, practice slow breathing during rush hour, and imagine hidden cameras uploading to YouTube when children make a mess. They find ways to show patience to others before they feel it. In time, their patient actions form a patient heart.

Generosity, humility, forgiveness, and kindness, moderation, courage, and compassion can all grow in the same way.

These ways of living comprise the way of Christ. They are our Spiritual Spanx. We begin wearing them more or less reluctantly. And while our physical attire gradually begins to conform to our body, our spiritual apparel works in the opposite direction. Our hearts and minds begin to conform to these outward ways.

We are disciples of Christ. Jesus sends us into the world to make disciples. In the same way that Jesus is making disciples of us, we are called to invite others to join us in Christ's own gracious way of living: the way of justice and mercy, the way of humility and forgiveness, the way of peace and compassion. Hearts and minds will follow in time. Theirs and ours.

Reflection Questions

- Think about some things that are second nature for you now that seemed difficult or awkward when you first began learning to do them: driving a car, playing a musical instrument, swinging a tennis racket or a golf club, casting a fly rod, or assuming a yoga position. Tell the story about one of the learning experiences.
- Tell the story about a time that you struggled with a spiritual practice or felt spiritually stretched by a situation. For instance, share a time when your patience was sorely tried, you wrestled with forgiving someone, or you strained to find compassion for another person. What were the obstacles to growth? What were the challenges and what did you find helpful? Be as specific as you can.
- Where is God stretching you now? In what areas of your spiritual life do you want to grow?

4

Learning to Let Go of the Cookies

Read Matthew 25:14–30

Like most of us, I have a few disjointed memories of my early childhood. Fragments. Isolated episodes with little or no context. I can't quite piece together a complete narrative from my personal memory bank prior to about age five. But some of those early memories endure and even still bear emotional freight.

For instance, I remember a preschool at a private home in a room above a detached garage. We lived either in Mississippi or South Carolina at the time. Each of us brought our own lunch in indistinguishable brown paper bags.

One morning my mom told me that she had packed freshly baked chocolate chip cookies for my dessert. As I remember it, I couldn't find my bag when the lunch period came. Then I heard a girl say to the teacher, "Look, I'm feeding Becky her lunch. She's eating it. She loves the chocolate chip cookies."

I didn't say a thing. Already then I struggled with speaking in public. Other children had discovered that my speech impediment made for an easy target. So as best as I can recall, I sat in silence and simply didn't eat lunch. But I remember feeling stung that someone had taken something that belonged to me.

With some embarrassment I admit that for years I would feel the same sense of violation and resentment every time something triggered that memory.

That's pretty petty, I know. To make matters worse and my own smallness even more obvious, I eventually recalled that Becky was handicapped, and the girl who fed her (and whose name and face I cannot recall) was doing an especially kind thing.

So you see, there's a part of me that sympathizes with the third slave in the Parable of the Talents. That's the misguided part of me. But I'm getting ahead of myself. Let's review the parable and then I'll explain why I can so easily fill the shoes of the third slave and why I hope to outgrow them.

Before going on a long journey, a man gives each of his slaves a huge treasure. One got five talents. A second got two talents. And a third slave got one talent. We're not really sure how much a talent was. Some say each talent was worth fifteen years' wages. The point is not the precise amount, but that the amount is almost unimaginably huge. Let's just say that they all got a gazillion bucks.

The master does not give the slaves a precise set of instructions. Instead, he gives them each an enormous treasure and expects them to make something of it. The first two invested and doubled the original amount. The third servant dug a hole and buried the whole wad of cash. Burying was considered the safest means to secure money from theft. So, when holding someone else's money, you would be absolved of all responsibility for that money if you just buried it.

Now you might at this point think of the third slave as a very conservative investor. His main objective might have been to protect the master's corpus from loss. But the slave's own words contradict this interpretation. When his master gets back, the third slave digs up his master's cash, wipes off the dirt, and hands it back to him. Then he says, "Master, I knew that you were a harsh man, reaping where you did not sow, and gathering where you did not scatter seed."[2]

Let's put that another way. "What I make and accumulate is supposed to be mine. You were going to just take it from me. So I didn't bother." This is precisely what makes the master harsh in the slave's view. He takes what doesn't belong to him.

In my lesser moments, that's just where I resemble the third slave. I presume that whatever I earn with my own sweat and accumulate with my own good sense I have a right to keep. If I want to give some of it away, that's my decision. But if somebody wants to take it, I can do whatever it takes to hang on to my stuff.

In other words, those chocolate chip cookies are mine to eat, share, feed to the birds, or just give away as I see fit.

That's how the third slave sees it. The master has another point of view entirely.

The master makes an enormous and risky investment in the slave. Everything the slave has in the first place belongs to the master. And the whole point of making the investment is for the slave to take some initiative and some risk to enlarge the initial investment. Burying the money defeats the purpose. It amounts to refusing to be the master's agent.

The master in this parable is God. Jesus's portrayal of the master-slave relationship echoes the second Genesis creation story. God formed Adam from the dust and placed him in the Garden of Eden "to till it and keep it."[3] In other words, God sent Adam—and sends each of us—into the world to make it grow and flourish.

We are to leave this world a better place than we found it. Not for ourselves, but for others. Whatever we make in this life is God's. One day the master will return, and we will give back whatever we have made of all that we have been given. And then God will regift it to others.

In the meantime, whatever we happen to hold is not really ours. It belongs to God. This life is a rehearsal for the final act

---

2   Matthew 25:24.
3   Genesis 2:15.

of giving all we have back to our Maker. So, practicing generosity in our daily lives prepares us for the final surrender.

And Jesus has some pretty high standards for generosity on this planet. If someone tries to take the shirt off your back, give him your pants, shoes, and socks, too.[4] Sell all you've got, give it to the poor, and follow Jesus.[5]

No one can take anything from you when your purpose is to give what you have away. And that's what it's like to follow Jesus. Remember, he said, "For those who want to save their life will lose it, and those who lose their life for my sake will find it."[6]

As Robert Farrar Capon puts it, resurrection is only for the dead. Following Jesus is about dying and rising. We die to self: to stuff, to status, to all of it. And when we do, we receive new life––given as a gift. We only lose by clinging to what is not really ours in the first place.

Life is learning to let go of the cookies.

Reflection Questions

- Locate yourself in the Parable of the Talents as the third slave. Why do you think that burying the talents is the best strategy? Does the master's response to this strategy seem harsh? Just? Unfair?
- Name the earthly things that are most important to you in this life. How do you feel about the suggestion that God has given you these things? Do you believe that God has given you these things to keep or to give away?
- Imagine giving away the things most important to you in order to cling most deeply to God. What would it mean to give away family, career, status, reputation, material wealth, and security?
- What do you resist most strongly giving back to God?

---

4 Matthew 5:40.
5 Matthew 19:21.
6 Matthew 16:25.

5

Speaking with an Accent

Read Acts 2:1–22

In Luke's account of the Day of Pentecost, the Holy Spirit creates the Church.[7] Look carefully at what happens. The story says loads about what God intends for the Church to be. It says loads about who God intends for us—the community of Jesus-followers—to be.

For nine days the disciples had huddled together in an upper room, praying. On the tenth day the Holy Spirit made them a new creation: the Church. And what they did as the community of Jesus-followers is unlock the doors, throw open the windows, and head out into the streets. God was doing something out there. They wanted to be a part of it.

In other words, they didn't do what church-folk tend to do. Many of us think of starting a church as erecting a building and inviting people to join us inside for prayer. We even put

---

7   Acts 2:1–22.

up signs, design websites, and pay for newspaper ads inviting people to join us inside the building. They can join us whenever they want.

Even when the Church engages the world, we use the term "outreach" to talk about it. Think about that word for a minute. Outreach. The image is that we reach out from inside. But inside is where we belong. Evangelism takes the form of making outsiders into insiders. One of us.

That's exactly how the attractional church operates. And the declining vitality of many congregations in America tells us that this is not a winning strategy.

No wonder.

The Church portrayed in the Acts of the Apostles is missional to its very core. These early disciples knew that God has a mission in the world, and that God has created a Church to pursue that mission. That mission takes various forms, but its essence is reconciliation.

That newly formed Jesus-following community engages God's mission from the very start. They pour out onto the streets in the midst of an ongoing festival to tell good news.

They did not demand that their listeners become just like them, adhere to their own strict code of conduct, or submit to their own interpretations of just how the world works. They were delivering the news. God loves you. And that love is active and powerful. That love heals your wounds, nourishes your body, forgives your sins, rebuilds your shattered relationships, empowers you to make a contribution in this world, and brings you peace of mind.

What you say matters. How you say it matters just as much. Sometimes, maybe even more.

The disciples delivered this news in a language that the listeners could understand. More precisely, they found themselves speaking in languages not their own. In the power of God's Spirit each disciple spoke each listener's own native tongue. They delivered the message of reconciliation not just by conveying a set of ideas or by constructing winning arguments. They connected with strangers on the strangers' own terms.

And there was something humbling about it. They didn't speak these foreign languages as expert linguists or native speakers. At least, that's not what the text suggests to me. Remember that some in the crowd said, "Aren't these guys a bunch of Galileans?" Others said, "These guys are loaded, and it's not even noon yet!" In other words, they spoke so that people could understand them, but they had a noticeable accent.

Like I said earlier, what you say matters. But how you say it matters just as much. Maybe even more.

We infer things about a speaker on the basis of his or her accent. Unlike tone and volume—vocal elements that can indicate a speaker's mental and physical state—what we attribute to a speaker's character on the basis of his or her accent has a great deal to do with our own preferences, assumptions, and prejudices.

Accents have played a significant role in my life. As a preschooler and then again in middle school and high school, I lived with my mother and my maternal grandparents. Post-war immigrants from Austria, my family spoke German at home. Outside the house they spoke broken, heavily accented English.

Any foreign accent would have contrasted sharply with my deep South contexts in South Carolina and then Georgia, but remember that this was post-WWII America.

We fancied ourselves a melting pot. We were all supposed to be the same. And a German accent carried a distinct stigma. There was something shameful about being the losers of the great conflict and something sinister about being associated with the bad guys. So, my grandparents' and my mother's accents were the source of ridicule at the hands of some of my childhood peers.

During the first few years of elementary school, my mother joined my father in tiny Louisville, Georgia, as they tried a go at reconciliation. I didn't realize it, but while I was in Louisville, I began to develop a very thick southern accent. How would I have known? An accent is an accent only when you're the outsider. And southern Georgia was shaping my speech patterns and pronunciations to fit right in. (Sort of, but that's another story for another day.)

When my parents finally split for good, my mom and I moved to Atlanta, where I attended Catholic schools. Within minutes of opening my mouth my new classmates made it clear that my accent marked me as a hick and a rube. They had already learned to pronounce "I" like midwestern news anchors and mercilessly ribbed me by repeating my long "i" pronunciation with cartoonish exaggeration. They thought I was a hilarious curiosity. Clearly unsophisticated, poorly educated, and perhaps a bit dim.

Atlanta—and my peers—gradually did its work on my accent, sharpening up pronunciations and substituting country usages like "ain't" and "yonder" with more suitable urban constructions.

But then a funny thing happened when I would return to Louisville to visit my father. He and my half-brother Joel would mock my new pronunciations as uppity and phony. Their criticism and condescension only increased as I advanced in education.

So here's a revealing thing that happened years later. My oldest son Andrew heard me talking to somebody on the phone. When the conversation had ended, Andrew said, "You were talking to Grandpa. I could tell because your southern accent gets really thick when you talk to him."

He was exactly right. I don't do it consciously, but my accent shifts depending upon my context. With professors in the philosophy department at Emory, my pronunciations and cadences will still echo their own sophisticated tones and rhythms. Back in rural Georgia, I think I sound a little like Andy Griffith.

Maybe my shifting accents mark me as a big phony. But honestly it's not something I do intentionally. The habit of matching my listener's accent started when I was very young, filled with self-doubt and the kind of yearning for acceptance and approval that comes from feeling excluded and deprived.

These days, something else is going on, I think. Connecting with other people motivates me. I thrive on being a helpful part of other people's lives. At one point in my life I was so afraid of rejection that I insisted that people meet me on my own terms. I didn't meet many people that way. So now I habitually seek to meet people on their terms.

You see, echoing another person's accent does not begin with speaking. It begins with listening. Only when I have genuinely heard the other person do I really have something to say. Only then do I know how to connect.

And reconciliation—God's essential mission—is all about connecting. What we say is important. What we do is probably much more important.

Just listen to what the world is telling us. Each summer thousands of children whose nutrition comes from the subsidized school lunch program will go hungry every day.

In the land that highly values equal opportunity, a family's earning power significantly affects the children's range of opportunities. For instance, your chance of finishing a college degree by the age of twenty-four is one in two if your family's income exceeds $90,000. But those odds drop to one in four if the family makes between $60,000 and $90,000. Once the family's income falls below $35,000 those odds plummet to one in seventeen.[8] In a country with an ever-widening income gap, this puts our commitment to equal opportunity at risk.

God sends us into the world to listen and to connect. That's what it means to proclaim the Good News. And as we go out into the world to engage God's mission, we do well to remember St. Francis's instructions to his monks. Preach the Gospel. Use words if necessary.

What we say matters. How we say it matters just as much. Sometimes, maybe even more.

---

8 I heard these statistics in the commencement address given by Dr. Paul Baker, Headmaster of Episcopal School of Acadiana in Lafayette, Louisiana, on May 31, 2014.

Reflection Questions

- Imagine trying to communicate with the crowd attending the festival on the day of Pentecost. Your potential listeners speak a variety of languages, most of which are not yours. Many of them have different political interests and even different theories about how the world works. How do you get their attention and hold it? How do you connect to them? How do you convey your message to them in a way that moves them?

- Tell a story about a time that you had trouble explaining something to someone else. What did you do to get your message across?

- Now tell a story about a time that you tried to get others to join you in some activity or course of action that was new. What did you do to persuade them to join you? How did they respond?

- Recall a conflict you had with someone who matters deeply to you. How did you resolve this conflict?

- What role did listening play for you in each of these examples?

- How does God speak to you most frequently? What do you do to listen attentively?

PART TWO

Family Scenes

And [Jesus] replied,
"Who are my mother and my brothers?"

Mark 3:33

6

Beggars and Saints

Read Matthew 5:1–12

After my parents had divorced—I guess I was around eleven years old—my mom and I lived in a car for a while. The little money we had left from her last paycheck had dwindled down to twelve cents.

One day we hadn't eaten by suppertime, and we couldn't afford to buy anything. So, my mom went to the back door of a restaurant and asked for some food. She came back with half a loaf of bread and a mostly full jar of peanut butter.

I don't remember eating. We surely did. We were both hungry. And I don't remember how my mom felt about any of it. She wasn't a proud woman, but she had always worked hard for a living. In fact, she got back to work as soon as she could find a job and literally worked until the very day she died. Her life's purpose was to provide for me. It had to have been demoralizing for her to admit to me that she couldn't buy food and humiliating for her to beg strangers for a handout.

We don't use the term "beggar" much these days. It seems harsh and condescending to our ears. The word "panhandling" has taken its place in some quarters, but that word's connotation is no less pejorative. People ask for assistance. In urban areas, they sometimes position themselves near busy doorways or metro stations. People seeking assistance frequently find their way to the doors of our churches.

Some of these people are homeless. They've lost a job or succumbed to addiction or, due to prolonged illness, have fallen hopelessly behind on the bills. A number of our homeless neighbors are mentally ill.

Others seeking assistance have hit a temporary rough spot and just need a little help to get back on their feet. There are a few who have always lived on welfare and have never learned a different way to get by in the world. Fewer still are just stinkers looking to take advantage of naive generosity.

Giving alms is a longstanding Christian practice. Jesus emphasizes it. The Hebrew Scriptures urge it. We see ourselves as those who have plenty. From our abundance, we hear God calling us to be merciful to those who suffer deprivation.

And yet, when we begin to see ourselves as benefactors, we have completely missed the point.

While Jesus wants us to continually stretch the limits of our generosity, he warns us to steer clear of thinking of ourselves as benefactors. Instead, he teaches us to be beggars at our very core.

Jesus says, "Blessed are the poor in spirit, for theirs is the kingdom of heaven."[9]

The Greek word used for "poor" in this translation means "beggar" in different contexts. So, here's what Jesus is saying: Blessed are the spiritual beggars, for they are filled with God's presence. Their emptiness makes room for God to pour himself into their lives. Holy people—saints—are God-saturated people because they have gotten themselves out of the way.

9 Matthew 5:3.

When spiritual beggars give, they give from the overflow. God's grace and tender mercy spills out from them, because they do not seek to retain for themselves what has been freely given to them. And crucially, their giving is always a reciprocal sharing among equals. Spiritual beggars pour out and drink in from each other the mercies of God that each brings to the other. There is no condescension.

By contrast, benefactors condescend when they give. Benefactors have spent their lives accumulating under the false impression that we are all entitled to keep as our own whatever we have gathered. Benefactors let go of a portion of their stockpiles to less fortunate people, with the emphasis on less.

Mind you, this is frequently an unwitting attitude, and the giving is done with a genuine desire to help. And yet, when we understand ourselves as benefactors, we have forgotten that all that we have is a divine gift. And crucially, we will entirely miss the truth that we are entering into partnership with a fellow beggar.

Outreach programs frequently function on a benefactor-recipient model. Some congregations send checks, and such generosity is good. But giving money can also keep us at a distance from the recipient.

Mission trips to impoverished locations bring us face to face with others. And yet, we often build homes, offer medical aid, or run a Vacation Bible School for a short period without sharing an equal, reciprocal partnership to engage God's mission. We can drive to another part of town to feed or clothe or even shelter strangers without genuinely making them our neighbor and joining them as partners in God's mission.

Benefactors keep a distance. Spiritual beggars meet neighbors and form partnerships.

The poor in spirit are spiritual beggars. They may in fact be beggars for food, money, prescription medicines, or utility payments. But we can assume this spiritual posture whether or not we are in physical want. And to be clear, being materially poor does not guarantee a posture of spiritual poverty.

Spiritual beggars rely upon God for grace. We come with nothing. We need everything.

Spending time in personal devotions, worshipping with the gathered community, doing works of mercy, pursuing social justice, and living with moral integrity do mark people as God's beloved. As blessed.

But God's love has been neither earned nor coerced by any of this. The divine love is given freely. Those who receive it freely bear its visible mark. They inherit the Kingdom of God. Saints are God-saturated beggars. Paradoxically, these beggars have the most to give.

Reflection Questions

- Is there someone in your life, past or present, who exemplifies what it means to be poor in spirit? Tell a story about that person that reveals their spiritual character.
- Is it easy or difficult for you to ask for help? Do you feel obligated to repay the one who has helped you? Tell the story about struggling to ask someone else for help.
- Tell a story about asking God for help. Be as specific as possible.

7

Life Is Not about Trying Harder

Read Luke 1:26–38

My late father, Sam, had three sons: Joel, Joseph, and me. Born of my father's first wife, Joel is my half brother and five years my senior. Joseph and I share the same mother. Born three years before me, Joseph died before I came on the scene.

My father also had two daughters. Marsha is his oldest child, ten years older than me and daughter of his first wife. My mother bore Marie when I was three, and Marie died soon thereafter. They are an important part of my larger story, too, but they do not figure as the main characters in the portion of the story that I want to share with you here.

Instead, I want to focus on how I responded to being Joel's half brother. Without realizing it until many years later, I responded to my place in this family matrix by gradually adopting a spirituality whose motto could be summarized in two words: Try harder. In other words, I was a misguided Christian for many years.

Throughout my childhood, Joel seemed to me to be fit, athletic, handsome, slim, and gregarious. By contrast, I saw myself as pudgy, homely, clumsy, and shy.

When the three of us fished together in my father's little johnboat, Joel always cast his lures exactly where he intended and caught more fish than I did. By contrast, I alternated sitting idly while my father untangled my fouled line and enduring his irritation for hooking bits of his clothing on the backswing of my casts.

All of this made me miserable.

Maybe someday I will tell this story with the warm glow of nostalgia. But today I tell it with some embarrassment. My discomfort doesn't come from my catastrophically bad fishing skills as a boy. Instead, I recognize now that my misery was a product of my constant struggle to outperform my half brother.

Warranted or not, I perceived that my father preferred Joel. It didn't help that the two of them teamed up to make fun of my weight and my ineptitude at a variety of manly pursuits. To be honest, they may have been trying to connect with me in their own way. Whatever their intentions, I read it as condescension and contempt.

In my child's heart, I came to believe that I could win my father's respect, approval, and affection by getting better and better at the things he valued. Joel was the standard by which I measured myself. Is it really any surprise that I would unwittingly transfer this transactional approach to my relationship with my father to my relationship with God?

Well, that's exactly what I did. God became for me the heavenly father to whom I had to prove myself worthy and lovable.

As a child, my try-harder spirituality expressed itself in being a goody-goody. Well, at least mostly. With adolescence, this all began to change, so that with early adulthood, I became the smart, cynical, party guy. I was never going to get God's approval anyway—just as I had never really gotten my father's approval—so to heck with it.

By God's persistent grace, my heart was never fully in the smart, cynical, hedonist game. My desire to be in relationship with God in Christ grew while I ignored and even resisted it. In time, that desire grew strong enough to give me the courage to drop the smart-cynical-guy act and to have the courage to be vulnerable enough to admit my unquenchable yearning for God's love.

But old faulty lessons do not fade easily, especially lessons learned in earliest childhood. As I turned to God with renewed sincerity and ardor, I nevertheless retained my misguided sense that God was a father whose approval and acceptance I needed to win. And so, I threw myself into prayer, study, and ministries. I tried harder to be religious. This didn't stop once I was ordained. I offered more Bible studies, visited the sick more frequently, increased the number of weekday services, agreed to more diocesan work, and saw more people for one-on-one spiritual direction.

Eventually, Jesus pulled me aside and reminded me of his mother. Over time Mary's example corrected my spiritual vision. She showed me that life is not about trying harder. But neither is it about giving up. Life is about giving in. Giving in to God's love for us.

The Angel Gabriel announced to Mary that she was to conceive. Or more precisely, he said something like this. "Congratulations! You're conceiving as we speak!"

In response, Mary said, "How can this be? I am a virgin."

To our ears, influenced as they are by a thoroughly scientific age, this question sounds like this: This is physically impossible. Explain the mechanism by which a virgin can conceive.

Mary was not asking for a scientific explanation. Neither was she expressing doubt. She was admitting powerlessness. She was acknowledging a simple fact. Conceiving at that moment was completely beyond her abilities. And yet she recognized an invitation from God to be a part of what God is up to.

Mary could say yes to engaging God's mission precisely because she had no illusion that participating in God's work of restoration and reconciliation had anything to do with her ability to achieve something. Instead, Mary recognized that God sought something else entirely. God called Mary to say yes to what God could do through her––so long as she didn't stand in the way.

Paradoxically, God's strength works most effectively through our weakness. As God said to the apostle Paul, "My grace is sufficient for you, for power is made perfect in weakness."[10]

In other words, Mary acknowledged her own powerlessness precisely in order to say yes to God's power working through her. Or as Mary herself put it six months later when visiting her cousin Elizabeth, "[H]e has looked with favor on the lowliness of his servant. . . . ; for the Mighty One has done great things for me."[11]

What Mary did is completely unrepeatable: she bore the Son of God. And yet how she did it sets an example for all of us who seek to follow Christ. She gave in to God's power working through her. Each of us has been created uniquely by God to play a role that is ours and ours alone in the fabric of the creation. No one else can do what God created you or me to do. We gain nothing by comparing ourselves to others. Such comparisons lead only to condescension or despair.

Following Christ is not about trying harder and harder to please God. Instead, it is to give in to the truth that God already delights in us, and to give in to that delight, so that God's redeeming love can accomplish infinite beauty and immortal goodness through the frail and fragile likes of us.

Reflection Questions

• Put yourself in Mary's shoes. How would you respond emotionally to the Angel Gabriel's announcement? What thoughts would cross your mind?

---

10 2 Corinthians 12:9.
11 Luke 1:48–49.

- Have you ever found yourself working to gain someone else's approval? Or have you ever worked to avoid someone else's rejection or judgment? Tell a story that illustrates this.
- If you have learned to let go of seeking the approval of others, share how you arrived at this place in your spiritual formation.
- Do you sometimes fear that you must win God's approval? If so, what do you find yourself doing to gain that approval? If not, what has assured you that you don't have to do this?

8

The Vulnerable God

Read Luke 15:1–10

Seminarians from many different religious traditions spend a summer doing Clinical Pastoral Education, or CPE. There are a variety of CPE sites. However, most programs occur in a hospital setting. Even though these seminarians serve as chaplains and offer spiritual support to patients and staff, the educational point of CPE is to make participants aware of how their ministry style is affecting others and how ministry situations press our already well-worn emotional buttons.

My CPE supervisor set the tone for us—at least she set the tone for me—the very first day. Quoting a writer whose name I can't remember, she said that life is the accumulation of loss. For the first time a significant dimension of my life came into focus. I realized at that instant that the deaths of my brother and my sister had formed the unseen, and unspeakable, setting for my life.

My mother had three children: my older brother Joseph, then me, and then my little sister Marie. Joseph and Marie had been named for my maternal grandparents. Joseph died before I was born. And yet for years my mother told and retold the story of his death. She imparted her unresolved loss to me in a kind of emotional osmosis.

Marie died when I was still a toddler. I remember writing Santa a letter in crayon and leaving it on the front stoop. "Santa, please give me a baby sister." And I remember asking why the Indians killed my baby sister when I learned that she had died. In that era, Westerns dominated television and portrayed Native Americans in ways that we recognize as offensive and condescending today.

When my CPE supervisor said that life was about accumulating loss, I recognized why as a child I always got a defensive lump in my throat when people referred to me as an only child. Back then I couldn't say what I can say now. I wasn't an only child. I was a bereaved child. There was a loneliness deep in my heart left by the palpable absence of what might have been with my brother Joseph and my sister Marie.

Now this is all common human stuff. People we love die, move away, grow distant, or even turn on us. If there is a fiber of decency in us, we will feel compassion for someone else's grief. We've been there. We get it.

Jesus tells a couple of parables that tell us that God gets it. God's been there, too. God suffers loss. That's what the parable of the lost sheep and the lost coin teach us.[12]

While I'm suggesting that these parables tell us who God is, that's not the message that some of us come away with. On the contrary, some readers will make these parables about us. They will fasten on the word "repent" and assume that these parables are really about our tendency to stray and the need for repentance.

Now it is certainly true that we all break some moral eggs in life. The Gospel does teach us the importance of a contrite heart, a sincere apology, and a steadfast commitment to improved behavior. And while these parables by no means contradict these principles of the Christian life, they do not teach

---

12 Luke 15:1–10.

them directly. Instead, they tell us why we would live such a life in the first place. They tell us about the God who loves us by exploring the contours of the kind of love God gives.

Once we understand that God loves us because of who God is, then we can see that our repentance--in fact our whole life-- is a response to God's extravagant love. Too many of us labor under the misconception that we must repent and improve to win God's affections. But I'm getting ahead of myself.

Let's dig into the parables, get to know God a bit better, and then turn to how what we've learned applies to our daily lives.

There is a scandal right at the heart of these two parables. And that scandal probably accounts for why so many of us end up assuming that the parables are about how we humans should act.

Here's the scandal:

A shepherd loses a sheep. A woman loses a coin.

The sheep does not go astray. It is lost. No thief steals the woman's coin. She loses it.

And there's the rub. The shepherd and the woman clearly symbolize God. God suffers loss. Some readers are quick to talk about human sin and the need to return to God precisely because they find it unthinkable that God could lose anything.

But that is exactly what these parables say, and if we're going to get a glimpse into God's radical, self-giving love, we will have to take that very seriously. God suffers loss. Now this is not the same thing as saying that God absent-mindedly loses track of his children like some distracted parent at Walmart. On the contrary, God invests deeply and constantly in the life of all creation.

God knows the number of hairs on your head, the temperature of each star in the universe, and the heart rate of each hummingbird. And all of these things actually matter. God does not merely accumulate data about things. God enters into deep, caring, nurturing relationship. In other words, God is infinitely vulnerable to the changes and the chances of every nook and cranny of the creation.

While we're at it, consider for just a minute what it means to call God the creator. Strictly speaking, God doesn't need anything. God is what philosophers and theologians call self-sufficient. God is perfect, lacking nothing. The Creator is the Good, the True, and the Beautiful. Any good, true, or beautiful thing we encounter on this planet derives its fleeting goodness, truth, and beauty from God.

God did not create the universe out of need. Instead, it is in God's very nature to impart the joy of goodness, truth, and beauty to another. To imbue an Other with value and significance.

That is the very essence of love.

God's love is not a *reaction* to the qualities we have. God's love *initiates;* it imparts value and significance. Out of nothing God loves us into something marvelous and breathtaking. When for any reason the goodness and beauty that God imparts ebbs and fades, God grieves. The Creator mourns for what might have been. God suffers loss at any departure from the good and the beautiful that is envisioned for us.

When we participate in addictive and self-destructive behaviors, God suffers loss.

When we oppress the poor, marginalize those who are different, and visit violence on one another, God suffers loss. God is vulnerable to the agony of hunger, poverty, homelessness, and war. When the sick suffer needlessly because they have no access to medical care, God suffers.

Now we might at this point slide back into thinking that these parables aim at telling us what to do. And I will come to the application of this lesson about God in just a moment. But stay with the parables themselves. They still have something to tell us about God and about what that suffering love does for us.

Let's turn from God as our creator to the cross of Jesus Christ. After all, the parables of the lost sheep and the lost coin tell us that God seeks us out and finds us. And it is in the cross that we see this most clearly.

God does not sit at a comfortable heavenly distance and assess our handiwork. That's just what we'll think if we assume that these parables are about what we have to do to please God. These parables are not about what we can do, but about what

God has done and is doing in Jesus. God seeks us and finds us precisely in order to restore us.

The cross shows us that God's suffering is not passive. In Jesus, God becomes vulnerable to us, to all the worst we have to give. God's love is not a display of masochism. It is the triumph of love over violence, depravity, selfishness, suffering, and death. In the very flesh of the Son Jesus, God becomes the recipient of all that debases and defiles the goodness and beauty that God originally imparted to us.

And God does what God always does. The Creator imparts new life. New value. New significance. In the resurrection, God more than restores the creation and the children of God. The Holy One makes a New Heaven and a New Earth, and God makes each of us a New Creation.

Let's face it. The New Heaven and the New Earth are a work in progress.

People still suffer and die from treatable illnesses because the medical care they need is inaccessible. Governments like Syria gas their citizens, and movements like ISIS terrorize and torture their perceived enemies. The history of racism in our country is still a living legacy, not just a wretched memory.

And as New Creations go, there's apparently a fair amount of assembly required. Our impulse to serve can still be at odds with our impulse for self-promotion. Self-preservation and self-giving still strive to have the loudest voice among our passions.

The point is not to change the world or change ourselves. Instead, the point is to live our lives as if we really believe that God is changing the world and changing us. Know that God is actively loving you, and make that knowledge real by loving your neighbor.

Here are some specific ways that the Gospel teaches us to do that:

Be a Jesus-following community that welcomes the stranger. And remember, the stranger is just the one that seems like a square peg to the round hole you keep trying to offer him or her. In some congregations that may be a gun-toting Republican, just as it could be a homeless alcoholic, a black Democrat, or a transgendered teenager in other congregations.

Learn to admit that your money and your possessions are not really yours. God gave you all of this to give away for the sake of the Kingdom.

Get yourselves out of the building and onto the streets. Stop trying to get people into the church and start taking the church to the people. Use your hands to take blood pressures, feed the hungry, and offer communion to the homeless on the sidewalk.

None of this will make God love you any better. The scandal is that God already loves us and remains vulnerable to losing us every day. We draw closest to God when we love one another.

Reflection Questions

- Think of the losses you have experienced over your life. Make a mental list or write the losses down, briefly at first.
- Considering the list you have made, tell the story of a loss that especially catches your attention right now. It doesn't have to be a profound loss. Simply share the loss and what your recovery from the loss was like.
- Now consider which of the losses that you listed continue to shape how you see yourself, other people, and God. Tell the story of that loss. Have you moved on? If not, tell about the struggle. If you have, talk about the process of moving on and what it means to you to move on from that loss.
- Have you ever felt God sharing your sense of loss? What was that like? What gave you the sense that God was undergoing that experience with you? How has this affected your idea of God and your relationship with God?
- Have you ever felt that God was distant in a time of loss? What was that like? How has this affected your idea of God and your relationship with God?

9

Hesitant Little Faith

Read Matthew 14:22–33

I have always been comfortable in the water. My father made sure that I could swim before I could walk. He had been a sailor in the Second World War and an underwater demolitionist, the precursor to what would become the Navy SEALs. Water commands my respect, but it has never scared me.

Well, that's not entirely true. When I was about nine, I was sure that I was drowning. Water terrified me that day.

I was tagging along with my older half-brother Joel and his friend Butch Dollar. They are five years older than me and considered me an annoyance.

Joel and I had a rocky relationship for lots of reasons that I did not understand back then. Our father had abandoned his first family, Joel's family, in favor of this new family. My family. We were locked in a struggle for my father's approval (which is not to say his affection). I was a pudgy kid with a speech impediment and wavering self-confidence. Joel was thin, athletic, and good-looking. And he was by far the superior swimmer.

Butch's father—Rufus Wrens (and no, I am not making these names up)—was something of a slum lord. He owned a tract of land on which tiny, ramshackle houses sat on cinder blocks along dirt roads. In tiny Louisville, Georgia, that's where many of our black citizens rented their homes. People called that little ghetto Wrens Quarter.

Joel and Butch led me into Wrens Quarter, and slowly some of the children living there started following us. We came to a pond in the center of the place. Joel and Butch announced that they were going to swim to the other side, assuming that I would never be able to swim that far. I figured that they were ditching me.

I stood there watching them as they drew closer to the far shore. That's when I decided to jump in and swim after them. At almost exactly the midway point, my energy was completely spent. I started going under.

As I thrashed I heard the kids on the bank yelling. Calling out to my half-brother. Those kids couldn't swim, so they couldn't come out to help me. But they did get Joel's attention. Joel swam back to me and pulled me back toward the shore. He was livid. When he got to the shallow water, he dumped me on the muddy bottom and stomped off.

He might have said something, but I can't remember. The message was clear enough. "If you weren't such a useless idiot none of this would have happened. You're more trouble than you're worth." I was utterly humiliated. Being rescued made me feel like a failure. A complete loser. That's certainly how my rescuer saw me.

I thought about my near-drowning experience as I imagined the story of Peter walking on and then sinking beneath the waves.[13] Peter was a fisherman. He knew how to swim. And he was out on the water by Jesus's own invitation. Well, strictly speaking, Peter had invited himself, and Jesus had said, "Sure, come on out." Still, Peter was sinking in a stormy sea. He was terrified. He cried out for help. And Jesus rescued him.

---

13 Matthew 14:22–33.

The text doesn't tell us how Peter felt about being rescued. But I believe that one of the lessons of this all-too-familiar passage is that being a person of faith means to look to God for salvation. Not as an exception to the general rule of our own spiritual and moral competence and self-reliance.

Nope. It seems to me that faith is a habitual way of navigating the planet. People who look to God for salvation admit that we cannot live life fully and fruitfully without drawing upon a power beyond ourselves who is greater than we are.

I don't really know why, but this is easier said than done. We seem convinced that we're supposed to validate our own existence by what we do. One of our chief spiritual struggles, it seems to me, is coming to terms with the very idea that we need a savior. It makes us feel like, well, failures. Losers on a cosmic scale.

I wonder if you see Peter as something of a failure in this story. Lots of preachers and teachers say so if not in so many words. They tell us that Peter got out of the boat in a great act of faith and that he sank only because he let doubt diminish his faith.

It's as if Jesus said, "If you hadn't doubted I wouldn't have had to go to all this trouble. You'd be strolling across this water like nobody's business. What a loser!"

What Jesus actually said was this: "You of little faith, why did you doubt?"[14]

The message he's delivering is something like this: "I know you want to trust me. What makes you hesitant?"

We all have a hesitant little faith. Trusting God is always risky for us and sometimes downright terrifying. That's because God is asking nothing less than to trust him with our temporal and eternal life.

Trust is something we grow into. God does not condemn us for needing to learn to trust him. God delights in building our trust by being trustworthy in ways both small and spectacular.

Here's what hesitant little faith looks like in my own life:

> I don't have all the right answers. About marriage, parenting, or how to be a deacon, priest or a bishop.

---

14 Matthew 14:31.

Even my most carefully constructed plans fail to take things into account, make faulty assumptions, and have negative results I neither intended nor anticipated.

Every time I do something good for somebody else it's only an imperfect good. But it's the only good that I have to offer.

My good intentions don't count for much of anything. My motives are generally mixed.

I should practice saying "I'm sorry." I'll get plenty of opportunity to use it.

A lot of stuff in this world is unfair. It breaks my heart. I'm clueless about what to do about most of it. But I still have to try.

I suppose this doesn't look like walking on water. It's more like being in over my head. But that doesn't make me, or you, a failure or a loser. It just makes us people who are learning to look to God for salvation in the messy, joyful place that is our life.

Reflection Questions

- Imagine yourself as Peter getting back in the boat with the rest of the disciples. You walked out on the water and then Jesus had to save you because you sank. What do you think those other disciples are thinking about you? How do you feel about the looks they're giving you? What do you imagine that they are saying about you?
- Talk about a publicly awkward moment. Maybe you tripped in public, showed up to an occasion dressed inappropriately, discovered that your zipper was down, or had someone tell you that you have a hole in your pants. How did you feel about that at the moment?
- Share a story about a misstep or a stumble or a mess that you've made at work or school or in the family and that you could not make right. Someone else had to come to your aid. How did you feel about yourself? About the one who helped you?
- How do you feel about calling Christ your Savior? What is Christ saving you from right now?

10

Forgiving

Read Matthew 18:21–35

I remember bits and pieces of that day. Just a toddler, I recall playing on the floor with my mother, Trudy. She had bought some cheap plastic dinosaurs for me at the dime store (or the Dollar Store in today's language), and she looked on as I marched them around and pitched them in battles with my little hands.

It was hard for her to get down on the floor. She was pregnant with my little sister. Very pregnant. My mother and I were always talking about having a little sister, how we would play together, what to name her.

"Take your toys and play in your room." My mother said this abruptly. Maybe I argued. I'm not sure. The next thing I remember is playing with those dinosaurs in my room and hearing my father's loud, angry voice.

Some time elapsed. My mother came into the room, closed the door, and sat down with me. "It's okay," she said, "it's okay."

It didn't feel okay. There was something menacing in the air, and although that invisible menace sometimes receded, it would never vanish altogether. It always threatened to flood the air again.

Years later my older half-sister told me what she had seen from another room. Our father had come home drunk. He had struck my mother and knocked her to the floor. While Trudy was lying there, he kicked her repeatedly in the stomach.

My half-sister's account of that day connected some dreadful dots for me. Memory being what it is, I have no further recollection of that day or how it fit into the days that followed. Instead, I only recall being told some time later that there would be no baby sister. She had gone to heaven.

It took my mother almost ten years to leave her husband. She worked on forgiving her abuser for the rest of her life. I think I'm still working on it.

Forgiveness doesn't happen all at once. Especially for deep, enduring injuries to our hearts and our souls, we forgive again and again over time.

At first it seems like we'll never get past the horror and the pain. Forgiveness seems to be a moment-by-moment work, maybe a work we'll never even get properly started. But with time, we seem to be doing just fine. No bitterness or resentment or irritability. And then we hear a song from back in the day, see a movie that touches a nerve, or just have a vivid memory out of nowhere. The old hurt, humiliation, and fear come rushing back. We struggle to forgive again.

My mother and I are not moral failures on this account. Our struggles have not resulted from harboring grievances. On the contrary, they demonstrate how forgiveness actually works. Forgiveness can take time and perseverance.

Peter once asked Jesus how many times we have to forgive somebody who sins against us. I suspect that Peter had repeat offenders in mind. The "moral big-man-on-campus" that Peter takes himself to be, answers his own question. "Count me in for seven times!" That exceeded the expectations of the day, which was to forgive three times. Peter has a superficial notion of forgiveness. He seems to view it like a toggle switch. You forgive and move on, like turning on a light switch. Jesus sees things differently. For some wrongs done to us, forgiving is something that we have to do over and over, going more deeply every time. These are the cases that will stretch our souls and expand our hearts.

That's what Jesus was saying with his response to Peter: "Not seven times, but, I tell you, seventy-seven times."[15]

Forgiveness has nothing to do with making excuses or letting people off the hook. Without honestly holding someone accountable, there is no forgiveness. Refusing to retaliate is the beginning of forgiveness. But only the beginning.

The destination of forgiveness is reconciliation. Now reconciliation is a two-way street, and it does require genuine contrition and amendment of life on the part of the wrongdoer. But it also requires something very costly from the injured person.

The cost of forgiveness is something like this. We recognize that even the one who has hurt us the most is not reducible to his or her worst actions and most offensive attitudes. He is redeemable, and God's own creation will not be complete without this person as a New Creation. My redemption is bound up with everybody else's redemption, even if I have to keep my distance for the rest of my life. We can't vote anyone off the island or throw anyone out of the lifeboat. And yes, that's costly.

But insisting on the prerogative to send our offenders into permanent exile is even more costly. And that is where the Parable of the Unforgiving Servant comes in.

To illustrate his point to Peter, Jesus tells a parable about a servant whom a king forgives an enormous debt. No sooner does this recipient of debt relief walk out the door than he encounters someone who owes him a relatively trivial amount. The servant blows his stack, throttles his debtor, demands repayment, and throws the debtor in prison because he can't pay.

15 Matthew 18:22.

The generous king hears about this episode. In response to the servant's refusal to forgive a debt as he himself had been forgiven, the king sentenced the servant to prison and torture forever.[16]

Some insist that the king in this parable is God. The message they take away is that God forgives us and, unless we forgive in the same way, God will withdraw forgiveness and punish us. Given what Jesus has just said to Peter, this interpretation has serious problems.

The king in the parable refuses to forgive the unforgiving servant. And yet, Jesus has told Peter that you can never give up on forgiveness. No one is disposable. Everyone is irreplaceable. We can't throw anyone away because God doesn't throw anyone away.

God is perfectly aware that our inability and unwillingness to forgive is one of our chief spiritual struggles. We probably need forgiveness for our lack of forgiveness more than anything else. The God whose Son tells us to persevere in forgiving seems unlikely to solve the problem of our unforgiveness toward each other by threatening to withdraw forgiveness from us.

Instead, I think the parable says something more like this. Clinging to our grievances casts us into a prison of our own making, a prison in which we feed upon the poison of our own bitterness and resentment. Jesus dies on the cross to set us free from precisely this prison.

Which brings us back to my mother and me.

This is not a story that wraps up in a neat bow. Before she died, Trudy had moved past active rage and habitual bitterness. She no longer actively fantasized about her ex-husband's suffering and humiliation. In fact, she rarely thought about him at all.

My story is still being written. My father has died. The anger and bitterness of my youth gave way initially to a sense of loss for what might have been with my father. More recently, I've

---

16 Matthew 18:21–35.

been mining my heart and my memory for the imperfect gifts that my father gave me. In time, forgiveness will take me down different, unforeseen paths.

Forgiveness does not happen all at once. In fact, I've come to think that forgiving is not a specific act we do. It's a path, a way of living. It's the Way of Christ.

Reflection Questions

- Have you ever needed someone else's forgiveness? Tell a story of being forgiven. How did this change your relationship with the other person and your relationship with yourself?
- Sometimes we yearn for forgiveness that someone else refuses to give. If you have experienced someone else's unwillingness to forgive you, share the story. How is this affecting your relationship with the other person? Your sense of yourself?
- Talk about a time that you struggled to forgive someone. Describe the process you went through. What made forgiving difficult? What motivated you to keep working on forgiveness? What did you find helpful in moving forward in the process of forgiveness? Has your forgiveness of the other person changed your relationship? Changed you?

PART THREE

Mothers and Daughters

We were her kids, her comrades, the end of her and the beginning. We took turns riding shotgun with her in the car. "Do I love you this much?" she'd ask us, holding her hands farther apart. "No," we'd say, with sly smiles. "Do I love you this much?" she'd ask again, and on and on and on, each time moving her hands farther apart. But she would never get there, no matter how wide she stretched her arms. The amount that she loved us was beyond her reach. It could not be quantified or contained. It was the ten thousand named things in the Tao Te Ching's universe and then ten thousand more. Her love was full-throated and all-encompassing and unadorned. Every day she blew through her entire reserve.

Cheryl Strayed, *Wild: From Lost to Found on the Pacific Crest Trail*[17]

---

17 New York: Alfred A Knopf, 2013.

11

Making a Holy Mess

Read Luke 2:1–7

After our daughter Meredith was born, our pediatrician came by the birthing room for a first checkup. The doctor told us, "She's perfect." Well, I could have told her that. Joy and I had already begun the misguided journey that many parents take.

We assumed that our daughter was perfect and that our role was to do whatever was necessary to keep from messing her up. All of our energies were to be devoted to building on and protecting her perfection.

It was only a matter of months before we discovered how misguided we had been. Another pediatrician in the same practice discovered an irregular heartbeat and referred us to a pediatric cardiologist. He told us, "She has a hole in her heart. She needs open-heart surgery." She was not perfect.

That was the beginning of our most significant lesson in parenting, in love, in being human. As it turns out, it's also one of the lessons in following Christ.

To paraphrase Brené Brown, we are all born imperfect. And each of us is going to stay that way. Moreover, we are all hardwired for struggle. We will make mistakes, get our hearts broken, take wrong turns, disappoint ourselves, let other people down, suffer loss, and wonder when the rest of the world will discover what a fraud we are.

Joy and I discovered that our mission as parents is not to apply successful parenting techniques in order to produce perfect, happy children. Instead, you might summarize our parenting mission this way: get connected and stay that way no matter what. Suit up, show up, and love that kid no matter what the day throws at you, what that kid throws at you, or how any of this is going to make you feel.

Strictly speaking, that's the core human mission. God sent us into this messy world to connect, to have the courage and the grace to keep loving in the face of uncertainty. To dare to accept the emotional exposure that connection with someone else always brings with it.

That is the message of the manger.[18] The Creator fashioned us as the image of God. In the birth of Jesus we see that God is all about connection. But how God connects might surprise you.

Some tell the story like this:

God created us to be perfect. After all, the perfect God could not possibly get the divine hands dirty with anyone less than perfect. We turned out to be quite a disappointment. We positively reek of imperfection. So, to salvage our relationship, God sent Jesus to clean us up, to make us presentable, to make us perfect so that God could bear the sight of us.

The manger tells a different story about God and about us:

God did not make us to be perfect. The Creator made us to be holy, to live into the divine image. God is love, and so love is the point of human life. And just in case you haven't noticed, love is messy. Jesus didn't come to clean up the mess. He came to make it holy. To make it the holy mess God had in mind in the first place.

Let me explain.

---

18 Luke 2:1–20.

Being human is a challenge. Being fully human—living a life marked by joy and creativity, a life awash in meaning and energized by purpose—we have to love in a way that resembles how God loves.

The manger tells us exactly what that looks like.

God doesn't lack anything, so God is not trying to fill some hole in the divine heart with somebody else's approval or applause or comfort. In other words, God doesn't become a human in order to get from us the love that God craves.

Instead, God reaches out to us to give us the love that we need. It's risky business.

After all, to connect with us, God became vulnerable. Our lives are uncertain. We laugh and we cry. We know tender intimacy and lonely isolation. Joy will fill our heart to bursting and sorrow will break it. We must choose a path without knowing all of its twists and turns or even precisely what the destination will look like.

When God connects with us, God is exposed emotionally to the full depth and breadth of our lives. God, you see, is love. And that's precisely what love means. To commit yourself so thoroughly to someone else's life that your own happiness is forever bound up with his or her life.

This is a challenge for us. That's because you can love like this only when you already feel worthy of love and belonging. People who experience the greatest levels of joy and creativity, tranquility and love are the most connected, but they do not look to the people and the things beyond themselves to feel lovable and worthy. People who feel worthy of love and respect give love away without hoping to get something in return.

Here's the problem. Most of us assume that to be worthy of love means that we have to be lovable. There must be something about us that attracts, earns, or achieves the love we need. More than a few of us believe that you have to be some form of perfect to be loved. You have to be at the top of your career or at the head of your class. You have to be sexy, well dressed, athletically exceptional, financially successful, or on the front cover of *People* magazine.

Or at least, you have to be good enough not to be at the bottom of the heap.

Whether we're burdened with perfectionism or just striving to be good enough on some scale, rejection waits in the wings. As long as we think of love as something that we have to attract, we will always be haunted by the thought that we may one day no longer be attractive enough to be worthy of love.

It doesn't really do any good to say that you have to love yourself first. Love doesn't work that way. Love is something that we always receive from someone beyond ourselves. It's about connection with another. Belonging to another by the other's full assent.

In the manger, Jesus tells us that we belong to him simply because he wants it that way. He loves us first so that we can love only as the beloved can.

Love is messy business. Imperfect beings connecting to each other heart to heart. God designed our lives to be just this kind of holy mess. To be honest, we have made our life an unholy mess in a myriad of ways. But Luke's birth narrative highlights one such way in particular.

We have to go back a few verses in the story to the pregnant Mary. She outlines our predicament and tells us what God is doing about it in the baby she carries in her womb.

> He has shown the strength of his arm,*
>   he has scattered the proud in their conceit.
> He has cast down the mighty from their thrones,*
>   and has lifted up the lowly.
> He has filled the hungry with good things,*
>   and the rich he has sent away empty.[19]

We are all in this together. From God's perspective, there is no distinction between mighty and lowly. That is all our doing. We carve the world up into mighty and lowly by narrowly pursuing our self-interest. In other words, we think that we have succeeded, that we have done well, when we make a better place for ourselves in the world even when others suffer want, loneliness, hunger, ignorance, and oppression.

---

19 From *The Magnificat* (Luke 1:51–53), as written in the Book of Common Prayer, 91.

In Jesus, God became one of the lowly. The Holy One leaned into the suffering, the pain, the violence, and the hunger, not just to experience the misery, but to transform it into joy, peace, and contentment. And that is exactly what God wants us to do. To seek to make the world a better place for us all.

God wants us to lead with our hearts, just as God does in Jesus. Our full plate makes us mindful of another's hunger. The roof over our head reminds us that some are homeless. When we struggle to find a place for one more book on our bookshelves, we think of those who cannot read. At the gym we remember that some suffer from untreated high blood pressure or diabetes.

We don't feel guilty. We feel gratitude and compassion. Our hearts break. Our hearts grow. We change the world. It's messy business. But it's a holy mess.

Reflection Questions

- Imagine the manger, but don't be romantic about it. Picture the dirt floor, the animal smells, and the hay carelessly strewn about. How do you feel about sitting on the floor? How would you feel about serving dinner to your children or your friends there? Now think about what it would be like to give birth there. Share your thoughts and feelings.

- Does your life sometimes feel like a mess? If it doesn't seem so to you, how would you respond if someone told you that is how it looks to them? If your life does seem like this, can you be comfortable inviting someone in just the way it is? What would it take for you to become comfortable?

- How do you respond to other people's messy homes, wardrobes, cars, families, or lives? Do you want to show them how to clean up? Do you reveal your messiness to them and sympathize? Are you able to laugh?

- Talk about a time when your life felt like a mess and you couldn't clean it up. Were you able to share your life's messiness and your feelings about it with others? What was that like? Did you sense God's presence?

12

Untroubled Hearts

Read John 14:1–14

Hearts figure prominently in my personal narrative.

My daughter Meredith underwent open heart surgery to repair a hole in her heart when she was just a toddler.

While Meredith was still a preschooler and Patrick was loitering in Joy's womb, my mother Trudy had a cardiac arrest. She fell to the floor behind the deli counter where she worked and died instantly.

When I was a preschooler and again starting in middle school, my mom and I lived with my maternal grandparents. My grandmother Marie stayed at home because she had what people back then called a weak heart. The common wisdom of the day warned her against exerting herself. From time to time she would have heart spells that forced her to lie on the sofa and place a glycerine tablet under her tongue.

There's something ironic about these three women. Each of them had some challenge with her physical heart. And yet when I think about what it means to live wholeheartedly, my daughter, my mother, and my grandmother come instantly to mind.

When the biblical writers refer to the heart, they have in mind a spiritual reality: the very center of our being. While they may have located that function deep within the human breast, they did not reduce it to the physiological processes of the heart as an organ.

Our mind, our emotions, our passions, and our will all intersect in the heart. We live not merely because the heart pumps blood. Instead, we get out of bed in the morning, persevere through adversity, sacrifice temporary pleasures, seek the well-being of others, dance for joy, weep with sorrow, and laugh until we cry because we have set our hearts on something. On someone.

That's what hearts do. They draw the very meaning of our existence by setting themselves on, by devoting themselves to, by relying utterly upon something beyond themselves. In other words, the heart inevitably seeks a god in whom to find rest.

Jesus is thinking of the heart along these lines when he says to his disciples, "Let not your heart be troubled."[20]

Now when we twenty-first-century Americans think of people having a troubled heart, many of us think that they are sad or anxious. In the contemporary imagination, the heart is the seat of our emotions. We also have difficulty seeing the value of hard emotions like grief and sorrow. So, it is not surprising that some of us hear Jesus's words to mean something like this: "Don't cry! It will be okay! You have to have faith."

As for me, I can't imagine Jesus saying to the Nigerian parents whose daughters have been kidnapped by the Jihadist group Boko Haram, "Stop feeling scared and miserable! Where's your faith?"

Or closer to my own home, a young couple just home for summer from their freshman year in college died in a fiery car

20 John 14:1.

crash in Shreveport. Can you really imagine Jesus saying to their parents, "Feeling grief is selfish. They're in heaven." Or worse, "Everything happens for a reason."

From everything the Gospels tell us about Jesus I don't believe that he would say any such thing. Instead, I suspect that he would sit down in the dust with any of us when life had laid us flat on our backs. He wouldn't say, "Don't feel that way." He didn't say it to his disciples the very night before his crucifixion. What he said was, "Let not your hearts be troubled."[21]

Or, to put it another way: Don't lose heart.

Don't let fear or grief or disappointment or pain make you withhold yourself, make you halfhearted. Be the wholehearted person God created you to be.

And being wholehearted brings us back to those three women with whom we began: my daughter Meredith, my mother Trudy, and my grandmother Marie. Each of them displays a dimension of what it means to be wholehearted.

On the day following her open heart procedure, Meredith was taking only Tylenol, and that was just to keep her temperature at normal levels. She kept sliding out of the bed. On her stomach and the incision on her chest! Finally, her nurse gave her a portable monitor so we could just let Meredith run up and down the hall laughing at her relieved and horrified parents.

Now a young woman, Meredith overflows with life in fits of laughter. She cuddles mangy dogs, and in her arms they somehow become cute. Anyone else's good news sends her into giddy celebration. Meredith's arms are wide open to life's goodness. To God's goodness. Those open arms make her vulnerable. They also make her alive. That's wholehearted living.

My mother Trudy was wholehearted in a different sort of way. She lived through WWII in Austria with Allied bombs falling on her town every day. Neighbors turned her in to Nazi authorities for suspicious behavior, so she spent the last portion of the war in a concentration camp. Later, two of her

---

21 John 14:1.

children died: my brother Joseph and my sister Marie. And yet, when life would from time to time leave me in a dusty heap, my mother would pick me up, dust me off, and repeat this refrain: "Remember, tomorrow is another day."

My mother was never afraid to get her hopes up. She persevered through war, imprisonment, and a parent's unthinkable grief. Not because she felt powerful enough to make things turn out the way she wanted or smart enough to work an angle, she just believed that God would not let her down. Not that bad things would never happen, but that God could and would redeem even the most heart-wrenching circumstances.

My grandmother Marie simply had a different center of gravity than many of us.

Once, when an ambulance had come to take her to the hospital, she stopped the EMTs as they were wheeling her out of the front door. She remembered that mechanics had had my car for much longer than they had promised and that it had caused some aggravating disruptions in my life. She called me over and said, "It's not fair that they haven't finished your car yet. I hope they get it done soon."

This woman did not have a weak heart. At least, she didn't have a weak heart of the spiritual sort. My grandmother's concern for others was a habitual practice, not an occasional grand gesture or some theological principle. She didn't put it in these words, but she believed that when Jesus said take up your cross and lose your life to save it, he meant basically, "Get over yourself and you'll find yourself."

I tell these stories because they give just a glimpse of three untroubled hearts. They are not immune to grief, sorrow, or disappointment. On the contrary, an untroubled heart is a vulnerable heart. It gives itself away. To paraphrase C. S. Lewis, this means that—when a heart is what it is supposed to be, when it is truly untroubled—it will be stretched and probably broken.

But that is what God designed hearts to do. To give themselves away. And in giving themselves away, finding the God in whom they will know rest.

Reflection Questions

- Imagine being one of the disciples. Jesus tells you that he is about to be crucified. Then he says, "Let not your heart be troubled." What is your first response? How is Jesus teaching you to respond to his death?
- Remember a time that your heart was troubled. What sorts of things did people say to you or do for you? What did you find unhelpful? What helped you to carry on? Where did you find healing and new life?
- When is it easy for you to love? When is love a struggle for you? What helps you to love someone who has hurt you? Someone you don't like? Someone you don't trust? Someone who dislikes you?

13

Body Language

Read Matthew 25:31–46

My mother learned English informally by immersion. She entered America through Ellis Island from war-ravaged Austria speaking only her native German.

By the time I came along, her accent had grown faint. She navigated our English-speaking world effortlessly, but her vocabulary remained limited and you would never have sought her out for helpful grammar tips.

Her functional but limited command of English made writing a chore. That's why she favored sending greeting cards over writing letters. When I was away at college or studying abroad, a card from her arrived in the mail at least once a week. In her florid, Old World handwriting, she would sign each card, "Love, Mom." Sometimes she would add, "I miss you and love you." She never wrote a note longer than that. And yet, she always chose cards with lengthy poems or quotations.

For years I looked at those cards in the same way that you might look at cards. They're thoughtful. A handwritten note is the gold standard of thoughtfulness, and cards don't quite match that depth of personal touch. But cards do show that a person took some trouble to connect. They just didn't reveal as much about themselves as personally as a handwritten note might.

My perspective changed when my mom told me about her approach to card buying. She said, "I love you so much. And I'm so proud of you. I don't have words like you do. I can't say how I feel. So I spend hours looking for a card that can tell you what you mean to me."

My mother never rushed by the grocery or the drug store to grab a card. She studied them so that she could send me just the right message. Greeting card messages may seem too generic to be genuinely personal. They're written for a general audience. And yet, my mother had invested each card that she sent to me with her own sentiments. In her hands, the message was meant uniquely for me. She was sharing herself with me.

Once I understood the depth of my mom's personal investment in those cards, I realized that my response to them had been woefully inadequate. Similarly, God sends messages that are at once directed to everyone and tailored specifically for each individual.

Through the Scriptures and the sacraments, through natural beauty and the arts, God says things for a general audience. And yet, God also sends messages uniquely for each individual. God speaks to the crowd, but God also gets personal.

Some people get the message. Others don't. Some people realize that the message is from God. Others don't. And most interestingly, some people haven't the faintest clue that the message is from God, and yet they respond to that message.

In Matthew's Gospel we hear that God is sending a message to all the nations. "When the Son of Man comes in his glory, and all the angels with him, then he will sit on the throne of his glory. All the nations will be gathered before him."[22] In other words,

---

22 Matthew 25:31–32a.

God is sending a message not just to Jews or to the followers of Jesus, but to the Gentiles. To nonbelievers around the world.

Some of them responded appropriately to God's message. Others did not. And Christ judges them—sorts them into sheep and goats—on the basis of their response.

And here's the crucial twist for understanding what Jesus is getting at. Neither group of people had the faintest clue that God had sent them a message. But they were still accountable for their response.

To the sheep, the king said, "I was hungry and you gave me food, I was thirsty and you gave me something to drink, I was a stranger and you welcomed me, I was naked and you gave me clothing, I was sick and you took care of me, I was in prison and you visited me."[23]

And the sheep respond to the king, "And when was this, precisely? Could you give us just a hint?"

You know the famous response: Whatever you do to the least of my sisters and brothers, you do to me.

In other words, God in Christ sends a message to everyone, simply everyone, in the powerless and the needy. And Christ isn't just sending a group e-mail here. He is investing himself in each message. The sender is present in the message sent.

God then judges us in accordance with how we respond to the needs, sorrows, and sufferings of the people we encounter. When we feed the hungry, give water to the thirsty, welcome a stranger, clothe the naked, treat and nurse the sick, and visit those in prison, we are saying yes to Christ himself. Even if we don't realize it.

Conversely, we turn our backs on Christ himself every time we show indifference to human want and misery and loneliness.

Remember the Summary of the Law: Love God with every fiber of your being. Love your neighbors as if your own well-being is inseparable from their health and security, their peace and joy. And by the way, everybody is your neighbor.

---

23 Matthew 25:35–36.

Christians know—or at least we should know—that works of mercy and insistence upon justice for all people form an essential part of our walk with Jesus. In the story of the sheep and the goats, we see clearly that Christ has claimed solidarity with the needy and the powerless.

To love Christ means to serve those who go without, those needing medical care, those who seem odd or unattractive to us, and even those behind bars. To add to their misery in any way is clearly contrary to God's will. When we merely ignore the needy and quietly accept the conditions that contribute to their deprivation, we are rejecting Jesus himself.

Christ is sending us a personal message in each hungry child. We can see our response to Jesus in how we treat the handicapped and the mentally ill. Jesus himself suffers with untreated hypertension and undiagnosed diabetes, shivers in the cold with shabby clothing, and feels forgotten by the world as he languishes in prison.

Jesus is sending us a personal message using a kind of body language. The suffering bodies of each person on this planet house a soul inhabited by Christ himself. And Jesus takes our response to his message very personally.

Reflection Questions

- Imagine God telling you in a normal human conversation how he sees your relationship with him. What tone of voice does God have? How are you responding emotionally?
- How does God speak to you? Talk about a time when God had a message for you. How did you respond?
- What helps you to hear God clearly? When are you most ready to hear God's message?
- What makes it difficult to hear and to respond to God's message for you?
- Talk about a time that you struggled to hear and to accept God's message.

14

Wounded Beauty

Read John 20:19–31

"There's been a problem with Meredith."

That's what my then five-year-old daughter's Sunday School teacher told me. My heart stopped. I guess her teacher saw my panic, because then she said, "Oh, she's alright. She just did something inappropriate in class."

As it turns out the teacher had asked the children in the class to tell something important about themselves. Meredith enthusiastically said, "I had a hole in my heart. And then I had surgery to fix it."

Then, she leaned over at the waist, grabbed the hem of her little jumper, and hoisted it above her head to expose her chest.

"And I've got a scar! Isn't it beautiful!"

The look of relief on my face probably puzzled Meredith's teacher. I suppose she expected me to be appalled or apologetic or even defensive. But I was relieved. I had initially thought that Meredith had been injured or that someone had been mean to her or that she had gotten sick. Hearing that Meredith was still in one piece and still keeping down her breakfast eased my mind, but relief came from an older, deeper place.

Meredith had been almost a year and a half old when she had had open heart surgery to close a hole in the wall separating the upper chambers of her heart. The prospect of the surgery itself rattled my wife, Joy, and me right down to our toes. We worried about whether or not Meredith would pull through.

And as trivial as it may sound, we had also worried about what life would be like for her after the surgery. Meredith would have a scar on her chest for the rest of her life. The surgeon was going to use a cosmetic surgery technique to close the incision, but we wondered if Meredith would feel disfigured, unattractive. Would she be forever self-conscious about her appearance?

You've probably guessed the source of my relief. Meredith's show-and-tell performance that morning assured me that Meredith knows how beautiful she is. In fact, she had even then a firmer grasp on what makes her beautiful—and what makes other people beautiful—than most of us have.

Joy and I had fretted that her scar would be disfiguring. By contrast, Meredith knew instinctively that it marked her forever as a healed person.

She had been born wounded. The hole in her heart had formed while she was still in her mother's womb. The mark on her chest is a sign that she had once been wounded but now was made whole. And that is what makes her—and what makes you and me—beautiful. We are healed persons.

We parents make the mistake of thinking that babies come into this world perfect and that our parental mission is to keep them from being screwed up. The truth is that we will all struggle, our sons and daughters included. They will get banged up, weathered, and even sorely cracked just like we have.

Our role is to love them. Love is the only power that transforms a wounded person into a healed person. There is no such thing as a completely unscathed person. We are either wounded and diminished, or we are healed.

There is one catch, however. The love that heals comes only from a power greater than any of us. We can choose to let that power flow through us. But we don't have it to give from our own resources.

And that is just what Jesus is getting at when he visits his friends on the night following his resurrection.[24] Jesus is inviting us to join God in God's mission. Not just to our own children-- but to the whole world.

Jesus shows us the Way of God's love. He *is* the Way of God's love. That Way is not so much a path that we can walk on our own as it is a style that is recognizably God's: Jesus reconnecting us with God and with one another.

In other words, God is doing what still seems to an awful lot of people a kind of un-God-like thing. God is getting really involved in our lives. I don't mean that God is moving us about like chess pieces or whispering little thoughts in our mind just to get us to follow some big plan God's got for us.

God remains embarrassingly vulnerable to us. It's positively undignified. No matter how self-absorbed, pigheaded, mis-guided, mean-spirited, unkempt, or how indifferent we are, God just holds arms wide to us. No defenses. No prior demands. God leans in. All the way.

And just in case you haven't noticed, vulnerability hurts. But I bet you have noticed. Loving somebody always means get-ting wounded. Sure, they might betray you or reject you, and Jesus certainly got plenty of that.

But even at its best, loving the way God loves is going to leave a mark. That's because in Jesus, God is compassion without reserve. No holds barred. God embraces every ounce of sorrow, hatred, lone-liness, hunger, degradation, exclusion, oppression and suffering, disappointment, and rejection we have ever or will ever experience.

And that's going to leave a mark. In the case of Jesus, it leaves a mark in his hands, his feet, and his side. And those marks just point to the mark that all of this has left on his heart.

---

24 John 20:19–29.

Jesus shows his friends the marks in his body to tell them what they could not have guessed. He is healed. He has endured the worst that the world has to offer and he is healed.

They would have had no problem believing that he endured the worst and that he was wounded, disfigured, and forever disabled. What he showed them instead was that he was healed and newly empowered to love in an even more earth-shaking way.

And what is that earth-shaking way Jesus is going to keep loving? And keep being vulnerable? And keep being wounded? And keep being healed? He's going to do it through his friends. Through you and me.

Jesus says, "As the Father has sent me, so I send you."[25]

Jesus's love heals our wounds. Jesus's love is not merely something we receive. It's a way of living that we inhabit.

And yet, Jesus doesn't heal us so that we are forever free, once and for all, from being wounded. On the contrary, Jesus heals us so that we are free to love. Free to be vulnerable. Free to be wounded again in the assurance that the love we are sharing is the love that heals the one we love and the love that heals us again and again.

We heal by loving with Christ's love. We are healed by loving with that love.

This is why Thomas balked.

Thomas said that he wouldn't believe until he saw the healed wounds. He didn't mean that he refused to give intellectual assent to the idea that Jesus is risen. He knew that Jesus and his friends were talking about walking a Way, about engaging God's mission in the world with their whole heart.

Serving the poor simply because they are poor.

Forgiving even the unrepentant.

Building bridges to dedicated bridge burners.

Visiting the lonely despite their "No Trespassing" signs.

Sitting with the outcasts, kissing lepers, and rubbing elbows with the disreputable.

---

25 John 20:21.

Before giving his life completely to the wounds that unguarded compassion would bring, Thomas wanted to see for himself that it was truly the Way of healing, not the way of pointless suffering.

And who can blame him?

So I suppose that's why Jesus showed up, not only once, but twice and again and again to his wary and fragile friends. He knows that he's asking us to take a big leap. To let ourselves get swept up in what he's doing, even though it looks pretty crazy.

That's why Jesus showed up that night and said, "I've got a scar! Isn't it beautiful!"

Reflection Questions

- Imagine that you are Thomas. Why do you insist on seeing and touching Jesus's wounds?
- Talk about a person that you love dearly. When and how has your love for that person wounded you? How has your compassion and empathy involved you in her or his struggles and hardships?
- Talk about a wound from which you have been healed. How did the healing take place? Was it sudden or gradual? How did the healing make you more than you were before you were wounded?
- Talk about a wound from which you are still healing. Do you sense God at work in your woundedness? Does God seem absent? What do you fear that this wound will leave you? Where do you hope it will take you?

15

Looking for the Keys

Matthew 16:13–20

Autism Spectrum Disorder occurs in one out of sixty-seven people. As the word "spectrum" suggests, autism expresses itself across a range of severity. My daughter Meredith is at the high-functioning end of that spectrum.

We all know quirky, socially awkward people who otherwise function well at work and at home. They may have especially sharp intellects, play a mean jazz piano, or solve intricate puzzles in a snap. They may offend others with their blunt observations, make seemingly irrelevant contributions to a conversation, or relate a story or give an explanation in excruciating detail without realizing that everyone else has stopped listening.

Some of these folks are on the autism spectrum.

They differ in degree of severity from others who might fit our preconceptions about autism. There is no rocking. No obsessive ritual behavior. Far from nonverbal, many of them will talk your ear off and will even look you in the eye.

But everyone on the autism spectrum shares this: they struggle with making connections with other people. It's not that they don't want to form bonds of affection and mutual understanding. On the contrary, those with high functioning autism often yearn to be known and loved, to have companionship and understanding. But the way their brains are wired makes it very difficult for them to read other people. It's as if they lack the key to unlock the code of facial expressions, body language, vocal tone, and speech volume that most of us apply automatically in reading each other. The problem is not that they don't see these communication clues. Instead, they lack the key to break the code and arrive at the meaning.

Here's an analogy. Imagine approaching a stop sign as you travel along a road. Without thinking, your foot hovers over and then applies pressure to the brake. You may be thinking about something else entirely, and once you arrive at your destination, you may have no recollection of stopping at that sign. But that's exactly what you did. You understood the sign's meaning instinctively. You have long ago internalized the key to such a sign's meaning.

Now imagine driving down the road of a foreign land where all the signs are unfamiliar. It's not just that you can't read the words on the sign. The transportation department of this country uses different shapes and colors from any you've ever seen. You know that there are traffic signs, but you haven't a clue what those signs are actually telling you. Are you supposed to stop? Yield? Slow down? Watch for pedestrians or wildlife?

You need a key. You would do well to go to the Department of Motor Vehicles, pick up a driver's manual, and study the section about traffic signs (with a foreign language dictionary in one hand). You'll probably need to spend some time driving while you're still learning the key. Gaining a complete comprehension of the key involves learning the proper responses to the signs when you're behind the wheel. But eventually, you'll respond instinctively to those signs. Your responses will be second nature. You will have internalized the key.

Some people with high-functioning autism can learn to read people in an analogous way. And that's just what my daughter Meredith does. She is joyful and loves company, and she has for years been working very intentionally on social skills.

At one point she realized that jokes posed a challenge for her. People connect by telling each other jokes and laughing at each other's jokes. She had trouble recognizing when people were telling a joke. And she became aware of her challenge. So, she looked for some keys.

She started by working on how to identify jokes. People laughed. So she laughed. That's not to say that she got the joke. But the laughter—and the tone of the laughter—became for her a reliable sign that a joke had been told.

Next, she recognized that certain kinds of storytelling signaled that someone was telling a joke. Then, she began seeing what makes for a punchline. These days, she tells jokes. I suspect that she and I experience jokes differently, but we're able to share in jokes today.

She had found a key. And to be honest, I can understand her because I found a key. Instead of expecting her to process information like I do or respond to situations like I do or even try foods that I willingly try, I've come to recognize her responses as coming from a brain wired differently from mine.

And given her extraordinary ability to communicate with animals, to read musical scores and hear musical punchlines that go right over my head, I have come to appreciate that different is actually a very good thing. I just needed a key to connect with her in her difference.

Jesus gives Peter the keys to the Kingdom of Heaven. The keys to connecting with everyone, especially those with whom we struggle most to feel compassion and empathy. The keys to loving our neighbor as ourself when our neighbor seems to have landed from a distant planet, a planet to which we might wish that they would soon return.

Sometimes we call that person the other, or the stranger, or a foreigner. Sometimes we call that person an enemy. Jesus relentlessly insists that we learn to call that person neighbor, and sibling, and friend.

We sometimes meet difference with condescension and contempt. There are plenty of disparaging terms for blacks, whites, Latinos, and Cajuns. And these slurs betray an ungenerous attitude of the heart. Jesus is clear. "If you insult a brother or sister, you will be liable to the council; and if you say, 'You fool', you will be liable to the hell of fire."[26]

In the Kingdom of Heaven, we are stretched and enriched by each other's differences. The key to embracing the stranger as friend, the other as sibling, is to remember that Jesus is always found in that other.

Remember what Jesus said about the poor, the hungry, the naked, and the homeless. What we have done for the least of his brothers and sisters, we have done for Christ himself.[27]

If our hearts are to be stretched enough to receive God in Christ, then we must let God stretch our hearts enough to receive others in all their differences. Especially the differences that stretch us the most.

Jesus gave Peter, and he gives all his disciples, the keys to the Kingdom of Heaven. In Christ, we are growing in our willingness to seek family resemblances in and among differences that we have sometimes used to separate us. The keys to the Kingdom enable us to read all people as the beloved children of God.

Reflection Questions

- Assume that Jesus has given you the key to the Kingdom of Heaven. What sort of key is it? What does it unlock? What does it lock?
- Talk about a time when you came to see that you had underestimated or unfairly judged someone else. How did you come to see that person from a different perspective?

---

26 Matthew 5:22.
27 Matthew 25:34–40.

- Talk about a time that you struggled to understand another person's point of view or life choices. What effect did this have on your relationship? Were you able to reach understanding? How did you do that?
- What kinds of people make you uncomfortable or put you off? How do you feel about your responses to such people?

PART FOUR

Film, Fiction, Life

There is something in us, as storytellers and as listeners to stories, that demands the redemptive act,
that demands that what falls at least be offered the
chance to be restored.

Flannery O'Connor, *Mystery and Manners:
Occasional Prose*[28]

28 New York: Farrar, Straus and Giroux, 1970.

16

Peas and Carrots and Creeds

Read John 10:22–30

Jesus told his critics that they don't believe because they don't belong. They don't believe that he is the Messiah because they do not belong to his sheep.[29] Now this is odd; at least it's odd if we'll really let what Jesus says sink in and confront the ways many of us normally think. Jesus has just said something about following him that turns a customary way of talking about our faith on its head.

Many of us have assumed that the first step in belonging to Jesus's flock is to confess your belief in him as your Lord and Savior. In other words, you have to believe to belong. But Jesus himself has just said that you're not going to believe in him until you belong to his sheep.

---

29 John 10:26.

Thinkers like Phyllis Tickle, Diana Butler Bass, and Brian McLaren have been helping us see that "belonging" and "believing" must not mean what we have thought they mean. So, let's take some time to think about how believing emerges from belonging, starting with what Jesus means by belonging.

In the movie *Forrest Gump*, Forrest's best friend and life-long love was named Jenny. As Forrest put it, he and Jenny went together like peas and carrots. They belong together.

Their relationship is no storybook romance. They met on the school bus as children. Here's how Forrest describes it:

> You know it's funny what a young man recollects?
> 'Cause I don't remember bein' born. I don't recall what
> I got for my first Christmas and I don't know when
> I went on my first outdoor picnic. But I do remember
> the first time I heard the sweetest voice in the wide
> world.[30]

That sweetest voice was Jenny telling him he could sit with her after no one else would share his or her seat with him. Forrest and Jenny belonged together.

They were not perfectly compatible. Forrest was mentally handicapped and socially awkward, the son of a single mother in the deep South of the sixties. Jenny was a gentle but desperate survivor, struggling to piece together a life shattered early by her father's regular abuse. Forrest was perpetually naive, and Jenny was world-weary before reaching her teens.

They were not like puzzle pieces to one another. Their lives were too ragged and uneven for that. But Forrest could not conceive of being Forrest without Jenny. And even though it took many miles, and more abusive relationships, drugs, desperation, and even AIDS, Jenny came to see the same thing. Jenny could not be Jenny without Forrest. Peas and carrots.

---

30 *Forrest Gump*, directed by Robert Zemickis (1994: Paramount Pictures).

That is how we belong to Jesus' sheep. Like peas and carrots. Not just with Jesus. But with his sheep. His ragged, plain, sometimes quarrelsome, often unspectacular sheep. We belong to the flock. Then we believe in the shepherd.

For years, churches approached the relationship between believing and belonging in exactly the opposite way. To be honest, many still do. They think that individuals must first confess belief in Jesus and can only then join a flock of like-minded people. They assume that belief in the Shepherd is the criterion for belonging to the flock.

Jesus doesn't think that believing and belonging work that way.

You would think that we Episcopalians know this already. Like many other denominations, Episcopalians baptize infants. We incorporate people into the flock before they can say, well, flock. Or Jesus. Or feed me. Or change me. They belong before they could possibly believe.

Now some parents and godparents act as if that's all that there is to it. You get the magic sprinkle and you're done. But belonging is a process. Believing emerges out of that process over time.

For instance, I belong to my wife, Joy, and she belongs to me. She's not my possession and I'm not hers.

We can anticipate each other's thoughts. When we're in the kitchen we share the work in ways that require no prior discussion. As a mental reflex I think about my time with her and the effect on her of any commitment I consider making. She's on my mind when I'm away from her and I want to share what's on my mind when she's around. Peas and carrots.

But we didn't get there overnight.

I remember the very moment I fell in love with her. Exactly what she was wearing, where we were, and who was present. I sensed that we were peas and carrots in the making. (She, by contrast, took significant convincing.)

That was over thirty years ago. Or more accurately, that was a long string of individual days. A string that now runs thirty years' worth of shared cups of morning coffee, morning walks, evening talks, grocery lists, chauffeuring kids, arguing and making up, Christmases and Monday mornings, child vomit, science fairs, and flat tires.

We suited up and showed up. Every day. Regardless of how we happened to feel about it at the moment.

Being me is being in this marriage. We belong together. I still have to choose this marriage every day. But now the force of habitual choice and affection, shared memories and shared dreams, shapes how I see the world, what I value, and the sense of purpose that motivates me. In other words, my belonging shapes my believing.

That's how you become one of the flock. Sure, God does something remarkable at Holy Baptism. And we acknowledge how far that work has come, and our devotion to stay at it, in the Rite of Confirmation. But we will still have to suit up and show up.

For some of us, becoming a member of the flock developed as we worshipped together week in and week out. Increasingly, people are finding alternative ways to belong. Making lunches for homeless neighbors, checking blood pressures as part of a mobile medical team, gathering for beer and conversation with a group of spiritually curious people at a local pub, or knitting shawls for people undergoing chemotherapy.

Over time, we develop what the Germans call a *Gemein-shaftsgefühl*. That's a felt sense that we belong together. We are known and valued. We are part of something greater than ourselves that would be diminished by our absence. And we could not be who we are without these other people. We are peas and carrots.

Believing emerges from belonging.

For instance, I believe in my marriage, in marriage generally, because I'm living one. Because of this I can begin to say something remotely articulate about marriage.

What I say is not definitive or final, but it's based in a lived reality. It is true, and it needs to be fleshed out and complemented by what others have to say as well. We will speak the truth together, those of us who are already living it as best we can, those who have had the heartbreak of failed marriage, and those with grace and courage enough to try it again.

We come to believe in Jesus the Good Shepherd as we belong to his flock over time. Belonging emerges as we engage with the flock in the practices that make the flock what it is.

Jesus's flock welcomes everybody, no exceptions. Injury meets with forgiveness. People give each other a second chance. And a third and a fourth and a fifth. Whatever it takes. Anybody else's hunger, fragile health, or homelessness diminishes us, so we feel compelled to do something about it.

Living a common life like this develops habits of thinking, feeling, and willing within us. As we reflect upon our common experience together, we express who God is for us and who we are together in statements like the Apostles' Creed and the Nicene Creed.

We don't use these creeds as litmus tests to exclude those who don't belong. Instead, we offer the creeds in the midst of our worship as the accumulated wisdom of the flock to which we belong, a wisdom that has been accruing for centuries. Like the prayers that we say in our liturgy, they're articulations of a faith—an experience of God and of one another—that we hope to grow into fully.

Believing is something we grow into by belonging. And that's one of the things that characterizes the flock of Jesus, at least when we're at our best. We recognize one of our own in everyone we meet. They belong to us and we to them. Like peas and carrots.

Reflection Questions

- Are you still wondering who Jesus is and what he has to do with your life? If so, share the questions and doubts that you have. If not, share who Jesus is to you and how you came to see him this way.

- Talk about a time in your life that you felt left out or out of place.
- Where do you feel most at ease and accepted by others? What is it about this group that makes you feel at home? How has your participation in this group shaped how you think and how you act?
- Do you feel a sense of belonging in church? If not, what makes you feel excluded? If so, what gives you that sense of belonging?

17

Losing Religion and Finding Faith

Read Matthew 6:1–6, 16–21

Flannery O'Connor's stories are full of religious people. People whose religious purity and moral rectitude would trigger Jesus's gag reflex.

For instance, there's Mrs. Turpin from the short story "Revelation." Serenely confident of her own goodness and of her good standing with Jesus, Mrs. Turpin scans and silently classifies the people who share space with her in a doctor's waiting room.

Black (using the n-word). White trash. Common. Ugly. In her own assessment of things, she is higher on the scale of human worth than all of these people because she is a good Christian woman.

In a manner of speaking, she is both good and Christian, at least to all outward appearances.

She works hard, pays her own way, and always says and does the polite and proper thing.

She goes to church, knows hymns by heart, and chatters with Jesus like a trusted member of the beauty shop gossip circle.

Religion has gotten in the way of her faith, of her relationship with God. Mrs. Turpin is an example of the kind of skin-deep piety and outward moral correctness that Jesus warns about in a portion of the Sermon on the Mount.

Here's what Jesus says: "Beware of practicing your piety before others in order to be seen by them; for then you have no reward from your Father in heaven."[31]

Jesus is not telling us to hide our spiritual practices from public view. He is not especially concerned with whether or not we will wipe the ashes from our foreheads following Ash Wednesday services or look over our shoulders before dipping our fingers in the holy water font.

Instead, Jesus wants us to be clear that God is in the grace business. Grace changes who we are. Too often religious people like Mrs. Turpin assume that God is just a bookkeeper, a divine bean counter whose only function is to add up the good we have done to see if we have earned an entry pass for the pearly gates.

Classical spiritual disciplines like prayer, repentance, Bible study, fasting, and almsgiving contain a peculiar danger for us. While they can draw us deeper into grace, they can also get in the way of our relationship with God. In other words, our own religious busyness can get in the way of spiritual transformation.

That is what happened with Mrs. Turpin. She is not presenting a God-fearing front to hide from others her devious motives or malicious intentions. She has not the first clue that her outer and inner lives stand in mortal tension with each other. In fact, it never occurs to her that anything about her interior life needs changing. She is convinced that, so long as she does all the right things, God will have to accept her. It

---

31 Matthew 6:1.

would come as a huge surprise to her to discover that God is more interested in who she is through what is done for her than in what she does to win God's approval.

God is more interested in who she becomes by his grace than in what she can achieve through her own efforts. And the same goes for you and me.

Strictly speaking, Mrs. Turpin gets just that surprising message about her inner life beginning with a confrontation with a character named Mary Grace. In the waiting room, the troubled young college student Mary Grace hurls a book—a book entitled *Human Development*—striking Mrs. Turpin on the forehead. Before being dragged off to an asylum, Mary Grace whispers to Mrs. Turpin, "Go back to hell where you came from, you old wart hog."

God, you see, is about grace. And grace changes who we are from the inside out and from the outside in. That change is almost always surprising, sometimes startling, and frequently painful. But it is always good.

Religious practices can be a vehicle through which God shapes us with grace, but paradoxically they will just get in our way if we approach them in the wrong way. That's why Jesus says, "Do not store up for yourselves treasures on earth."[32] In other words, don't approach the classical spiritual practices as a set of achievements that will win God's approval.

Instead, approach them as ways to make yourself available to God's grace.

For instance, those of us who follow a liturgical calendar observe Lent as a season of repentance. While this can include making lists of naughty deeds and admitting to periods spent as moral and spiritual couch potatoes, penitence boils down to something radical, something right at the root of things. Primarily, repentance is a posture of submission. A penitent heart yearns to be more than it can ever make itself and so surrenders to the only one capable of such spiritual alchemy.

---

32 Matthew 6:19.

In our very marrow we want to love God without distraction and to love our neighbor effortlessly because of who they are, not what they do. When we repent, we fess up to this ridiculous desire and relent to God's unflagging invitation in Jesus to fulfill it.

On the cross, Jesus peels away even our finest achievements, because even they fall short of the glory of God. We surrender our best there, not only our worst. Whatever we cling to will inevitably be less than what Jesus can give us.

In the resurrection Jesus gives us the new life that only God can give. He does more than repair a few faults and touch up the chipped paint of our character. He makes us a New Creation. Spiritual practices are meant to help us let go of the life that we can make for ourselves so that we can be ready to receive the new life that Christ is preparing for us. Spiritual practices are just that, the practice of being people made by God instead of self-made people.

Ironically enough, religion can get in the way of spiritual growth. We can participate in spiritual practices as just one more way to be self-made people. By all means, take up the spiritual practices that Christians have exercised for centuries. But don't worry about getting them right to please God. Trust that, in Jesus, God is making us right with him.

Reflection Questions

- How do you draw close to God? Are there any spiritual practices that you find especially helpful?
- How does your church help you draw closer to God? Does your congregation sometimes hinder your sense of closeness to God? If so, how?
- Talk about a time that you felt stretched by God.

18

Hoping

Read Matthew 25:1–13

One of my favorite movies is *The Shawshank Redemption*. I've seen it countless times since it premiered two decades ago. Tim Robbins and Morgan Freeman star as convicts in Shawshank Prison who become friends. Both Andy (played by Robbins) and Red (Freeman) are serving life sentences.

Andy is a former banker falsely convicted of murdering his wife. He arrives at Shawshank dazed and disoriented by the demeaning realities of life in captivity. Red is wise in prison ways. Convicted as a young man, Red had already spent twenty years in the notoriously harsh prison before Andy arrived.

Red teaches Andy how to survive in lockup. How to get contraband. How to avoid beatings by the guards. And how to head off violence by fellow prisoners. All of this Andy learns gratefully.

But Andy never accepts Red's fundamental survival principle.

For Red, there was nothing beyond the walls of Shawshank Prison. The only sensible path for an inmate was to learn how to work the system that Shawshank created. When the guards were looking, you followed the rules.

If you resigned yourself to the world according to Shawshank, you could make a better place for yourself in that world. Red had become the contraband dealer, arranging to have items like cigarettes, posters, and rock hammers smuggled in to other inmates for a bartered price. Some jobs were less strenuous and less demeaning than others, and clever inmates knew how to angle for them.

Red colluded with Shawshank. He became the man that Shawshank allowed him to be.

By contrast, Andy refused to be defined by the stone walls, the iron bars, and the dehumanizing practices of prison. No less than Red, Andy endured daily headcount, bland food, drab clothing, and enforced confinement. And yet, Andy believed that his own worth, and the dignity of everyone around him, derived from a world beyond those prison walls. And that's exactly how he acted.

One day Andy sat at the lunch table with Red and his other convict friends. He had just been released from solitary confinement. His offense had been to play a recording of an aria from *The Marriage of Figaro* over the public address system, piping it into the prison yard for the inmates to hear.

Andy talked to those at the table about the power of music. It reminded him—as it had reminded every convict in that prison yard on that day—of a transcendence, of something more and greater than the life they all endured within the walls of Shawshank. Music was the reminder that—all appearances to the contrary—there is an enduring dignity within human life, a dignity that no circumstances can erase.

Clearly agitated, Red asks Andy, "What are you talking about?" Andy says that he's talking about hope.

Red says this in response: "Let me tell you something my friend. Hope is a dangerous thing. Hope can drive a man insane."

Hope is a dangerous thing. Not because it drives us insane. On the contrary, it's the only path to sanity in a crazy world. Men and women propelled by hope refuse to be confined and controlled by all that is toxic and destructive on this planet.

Greed and materialism, consumerism and war, domestic violence and poverty, racism and sexual exploitation, wage theft and addiction, all distort who God dreams that we will be. Hope taps into God's dream. God's dream—God's mission—is to restore everything that has been shattered and debased. To reconcile us to God and all of us to each other.

God's dream becomes reality only when it is a shared dream. When we hope, we do more than harbor positive thoughts, we act. We dream God's dream with our hands and our feet. Augustine put it something like this: "God without us will not, as we without God cannot."

In the Sermon on the Mount, Jesus teaches us how to be dangerous. How to anticipate the Kingdom of Heaven even while the world is decidedly crazy.

Turn the other cheek, forgive those who injure you, and remember the human dignity of your fiercest enemies. God is dreaming of peace, and it has to start somewhere. Blessed are the peacemakers.

Give the shirt off your back to whoever asks. Our fear of scarcity is a slur against God. God already gives plenty. God's delivery system includes our generosity.

Serve everyone, especially the ones who make you uncomfortable or tempt you to judge. Jesus said that whatever we do to the least, we do to him. In other words, refuse to rank people as higher or lower. Trust in God's dream of a world where everyone is equal, everyone is respected.

God dreams of a restored creation, and God holds us accountable for joining God in this dream.

That is the lesson of the Wise and Foolish Bridesmaids.[33] Ten maids wait for a bridegroom at night. He is delayed. Five

---

33 Matthew 25:1–13.

have brought enough oil to hold out until he finally arrives. The others run out of oil before he gets there. Only the five wise maids enter the wedding banquet.

The bridegroom said something like this to the ones who are left outside, "You didn't live your life in anticipation of my coming. You just took things as they were and made yourself at home. You spent your life making a better place for yourself in the world and never lifted a finger to make the world a better place."

Living in hope is dangerous. Hope dreams God's dream and changes the world.

At the close of *The Shawshank Redemption*, Red has finally been paroled. Andy had escaped years earlier and left a coded message for Red to join him in Mexico. Breaking parole, Red boards a bus, and we hear his thoughts as he leans out the bus window and feels the breeze on his face.

"I find I'm so excited, I can barely sit still or hold a thought in my head. I think it's the excitement only a free man can feel, a free man at the start of a long journey whose conclusion is uncertain. I hope I can make it across the border. I hope to see my friend and shake his hand. I hope the Pacific is as blue as it has been in my dreams. I hope."

Reflection Questions

Read the Serenity Prayer aloud:

> *God, grant me the serenity to accept the things I cannot change, the courage to change the things I can, and the wisdom to know the difference. Amen.*

- Talk about something that is hard for you to endure.
- Is it something that cannot be changed? How are you making peace with that?
- Is it something that you could change? What are you doing to make a difference? Is something holding you back from

making the changes that you can? What would give you the courage to change things?

- Has God ever made a significant change in your life that you could not have made for yourself? Talk about how that happened.

19

No Regrets

Read Matthew 3:1–12

John the Baptist says, "Repent, for the kingdom of heaven has come near."[34]

Let's expand on this just a bit.

Take an honest look at your life. No excuses. No edits. No spin. Look at your behavior, your motivations, the thoughts and feelings you hide. Now consider where a life like this is heading.

Some people will say something like this: "I have no regrets. If I hadn't done all of those things, I wouldn't be the person I am today."

If the point of living were to make ourselves into something we're satisfied with, we might be able to stop right there. For some people, that is precisely life's point. We are the authors of our own lives, and the only critics that matter are ourselves.

---

34 Matthew 3:2.

But followers of Jesus look at life from a different perspective. The point of life is to love God with every fiber of our being and to love our neighbors as if our own life depended upon their well-being.

To put it differently, we are practicing to live in the Kingdom of Heaven. That's the point of all that we do: practicing to live where God is close enough to touch and where no one's dignity is ever diminished.

The Baptizer is saying this: The Kingdom of Heaven is actually emerging right in the midst of the blemished, beautiful, shattered, tender, horrifying, breath-taking world we inhabit. The Kingdom of Heaven has come near. Repent. Learn to recognize and nurture the Kingdom right before your eyes. Learn to live a new way so that you can welcome the New Heaven and the New Earth that God is already making of our world.

I'll illustrate what I mean with a piece of literature that many of us associate with Christmas. As Christmas approaches, some of us will pull Charles Dickens's *A Christmas Carol* from the shelf to read to our children or maybe tune in to one of the several film versions scheduled by the cable networks. It's a familiar story about a changed life, a redeemed life. The life of Ebenezer Scrooge.

The vehicle for Scrooge's transformation is time travel of a sort. And well it should be. That's because, at its core, transformation is about how our past relates to our present and to our future. Dickens makes the point in the person of three spirits who visit Scrooge in succession: the Ghosts of Christmas Past, Present, and Future.

Guided by the Ghost of Christmas Past, Scrooge sees himself as a younger man. A vastly different man. Filled with joy, surrounded by friends, and deeply in love. Faced with the decision between love and financial gain, Scrooge makes the fateful decision to pursue career advancement and material wealth at the cost of everything else, including affection and belonging.

This choice was definitive. It was the choice of a life principle, and it shaped Scrooge's life from that point forward. The spirits of Christmas Present and Christmas Yet to Come simply reveal the trajectory set by Scrooge's fundamental commitment to success, achievement, and financial gain.

In the present, Scrooge has excluded himself from the warmth of family, and his greed has thrown the Cratchit family into a state of hunger, want, and untreated illness. Visions of the past taught Scrooge what might have been. Powerless to change the past, Scrooge was left with nothing more than regret. Glimpses of the present show the wounded Scrooge discovering his own loneliness along with the painful awareness of the damage he was doing to an honest, hard-working family. Faced with the consequences of his own choices, Scrooge was beset by guilt.

Transformation came with visions of the future. Scrooge foresees his own death. We all die, and the fact of his death was not the catalyst for change. Instead, it was the manner of his death and the world's response to it. Scrooge died alone. Friendless. Leaving his riches behind for strangers to scavenge and not one soul to mourn his passing.

Upon seeing clearly the trajectory of the life he had been leading, Scrooge makes another fateful decision on Christmas Day. From that moment forward he would live to make the world a better place for his fellow human beings instead of making a better place for himself in the world. He reconciled with his estranged nephew, became a generous benefactor to the Cratchits, and committed himself to eradicating want and misery wherever he found it. Charity, mercy, forbearance, and benevolence became his business.

The key, you see, was not that Scrooge decided to make himself a better man. Instead, he decided from that point on to make the world a better place.

You might think that his commitment to the well-being of others made Scrooge a better man. And maybe that is Dickens's point. But it is not the point of the Gospel. The point of the Good News is never what we do. It is what God has done, is doing, and will do.

God loves us. It all starts there. When we follow Jesus, everything else is a response to God's love. We do not make ourselves better so that God will love us. Instead, God loves us in Jesus, so now we can draw on that love to care for our neighbor as ourselves.

That is the essence of repentance: to love one another as a response to God's love for us. God's mission is to redeem the fractured creation. God places us on this planet to join God in this mission.

Like Ebenezer Scrooge, we can each do this in our individual lives. But God wants us to do more. God has called us into communities, into congregations, to pursue a mission of love and mercy and justice as one Body.

And that mission is not just far away in Africa or South America. It's down the street and around the corner. No congregation exists for itself, for its own membership. God has gathered every congregation in order to send you into the world as Jesus's hands and feet.

Scrooge discovered the mission by learning to see what was right in front of his face: his fractured family and the desperate conditions of his own employee's family. Right in your city or town or village or neighborhood there is want and misery. God has placed you here to listen and to respond.

Put on your walking shoes and listen to the stories of your surrounding community. Do not wait for the Ghosts of Christmas Past and Christmas Present to sweep you off your feet. The Holy Ghost is already stirring within you. She will show you the truth and give you what you need to respond in the name of God who became a man, the incarnate God who died and rose again.

God calls us to repent. God is not telling us to change our lives so that we can be accepted. Instead, God changes our lives when we join God in changing the world.

Reflection Questions

- Imagine someone telling you to repent. What is your gut response?
- What does it mean to repent? Has your idea of repentance changed over time?

- How have you come to terms with your past missteps? Do you have any regrets? Is it just water under the bridge? Have any of your stumbles or detours led to new life?
- Where do you feel the world's pain? How are you helping to heal the injuries you find in the world around you? Is there anything preventing you from engaging in the work of healing and restoration?

20

Seeing Lazarus

Read Luke 16:19–31

Lots of us have imagined what it would be like to be invisible. And a variety of popular authors have helped us to run with that fantasy.

For instance, J. K. Rowling's title character in *Harry Potter* has an invisibility cloak. He wears it from time to time to fight the evil forces aligned with Lord Voldemort.

Sue Storm appears in the pages of Marvel Comics, or should I say that she disappears. As one of the Fantastic Four, Sue possesses the super power to render herself invisible. While hidden from sight, the Invisible Woman does battle with criminals, like Doctor Doom, who have their own super powers.

H. G. Wells gave invisibility a sinister turn in his novel *The Invisible Man*. The title character plots to use his invisibility to conduct a reign of terror.

This sort of invisibility exists purely in fiction. However, Jesus tells a parable about a very real kind of invisibility. His parable of Lazarus and the rich man teaches us about our power to treat others as if they were invisible and about how this very power always turns against the one who wields it.[35]

Let's take a step back and look at some key elements of the parable. Jesus tells us that there was a rich man with an eye-popping wardrobe who threw lots of lavish parties. As it turns out, a homeless man named Lazarus had taken up residence right by his front door. He was dirty, ragged, starving, and obviously sick.

So, what does the rich man do about Lazarus? Nothing. It's not just that he offers no help, that he feeds only his chosen guests, or that he keeps buying new clothes while the beggar at his doorstep can barely cover himself. The rich man doesn't even tell Lazarus to go away or call the cops to run him off. There is no sign that the rich man is acting from some sense of compassion. Instead, Jesus crafts his parable in a way that suggests that the rich man simply takes no notice of Lazarus at all. He never gives the poor beggar a thought.

For the rich man, Lazarus is invisible. He looks right through Lazarus. Or more precisely, the rich man is so focused on his own comfort and status that Lazarus fades into the background completely. Lazarus is not important enough to the rich man to warrant any of his attention.

The rich man does eventually see Lazarus. It happens when he finds himself in hell and catches a glimpse of Lazarus in heaven sipping a piña colada with Father Abraham in heaven. He doesn't actually speak to Lazarus, but he does notice him for the first time.

And just why he notices him helps us to understand more clearly how and why he made Lazarus invisible in the first place. Listen to what he says to Abraham: "Send Lazarus to dip the tip of his finger in water and cool my tongue."[36]

The rich man finally sees Lazarus because he thinks that Lazarus can provide a means to his own comfort. It is there that

---

35 Luke 16:19–31.
36 Luke 16:24.

Jesus gives us the key to how the rich man made Lazarus invisible, and how we can fall into the same dehumanizing pattern.

Jesus has come to inaugurate the Kingdom of God. That Kingdom is not some faraway place. Instead, it is a way of relating to God and to one another that has not become a full reality, at least not yet.

In the Kingdom of God, we never see someone else as merely a means to our own ends, as an instrument for achieving our own agenda. Instead, in the Kingdom we know each other and ourselves as God's beloved. We are each infinitely valuable, infinitely worthy of respect. That is why in our Baptismal Covenant we pledge to respect the dignity of every human being. We acknowledge that God already loves him or her, so that respect is already due each and every person.

Jesus teaches us to adjust our own lives for the sake of the well-being of others. The rich man adjusted his relationship with others for the sake of his own private well-being. His leading question was something like this: What's in it for me?

And now consider just where this self-centered approach got the rich man. You might think that the message of the parable is that God punished the rich man's behavior by sending him to hell. While it is true that the golden rule of hell is self-absorption, you will miss the point if you think in terms of moral rules and divine punishment.

Consider for just a minute the simple fact that only Lazarus has a name in this parable. The rich man has no name. Jesus is a master storyteller. There is no way that this is accidental.

The rich man has no name because he has no enduring identity. Who he is derives from what he values. His clothes, his possessions, the various outer trappings of a materially wealthy life define who he is. And when he died, he had to let all of this go. There was nothing left by which the rich man could be distinguished from anyone else.

Paradoxically, the rich man makes himself invisible. His self-absorption left him a "nobody" from the perspective of eternity. He wore fine clothes in this life and made himself a spiritual empty suit.

By contrast, Lazarus is somebody for all of eternity. Again, Jesus teaches us by virtue of the name. The name "Lazarus" means "God is my help."

Lazarus did not define himself by his achievements or his possessions. Instead, Lazarus identified himself with his utter reliance upon God. As it turns out, it is our relationship with God and with each other through God, that will pass with us beyond the veil of death.

The Kingdom of God is still a work in progress. There are many people who languish in the kind of invisibility that God wants no part of. Our mission as followers of Jesus is to make the invisible visible.

So how do we go about making the invisible visible? We begin by learning to see them for ourselves.

As a first step, learn to walk around. Listen to people. Discover what they need. Learn from your community.

Some congregations have started community gardens in response to what they've learned about their neighbors' hunger and the quality of their diets. Others have begun delivering meals to shut-ins and supplying groceries for those facing food insecurity.

Still others have adopted schools, organized regular health screenings, provided furniture for the displaced, and partnered with other denominations to offer low-cost clothing.

Not one single person is invisible to God. But those who are hungry, sick, and lonely can feel out of sight and out of mind. God calls you and me to see with holy eyes. To see God's beloved as beloved, and to help them know themselves as beloved.

That's the Gospel, and Jesus sends us out to preach that Gospel. Words are good, but hands and feet preach this Gospel best.

Reflection Questions

- Have you ever felt out of sight and out of mind? If so, share that experience.

- Think about whom you notice and whom you do not notice on a daily basis. What draws your attention to some and deflects your attention from others? Who becomes invisible for you?
- Who do you think is invisible in American society? What is your responsibility toward those who have become invisible? Do you identify with them or do they seem like strangers to you? Have you ever sought to make them visible? How have you done that?

PART FIVE

Growing Up, Sort of

That's me, trying to make any progress at all with family, in work, relationships, self-image: scooch, scooch, stall; scooch, stall, catastrophic reversal; bog, bog, scooch.

Anne Lamott, *Grace (Eventually): Thoughts on Faith*[37]

37 New York: Penguin Group, 2007.

21

Being Yourself Is Not All about You

Read Matthew 3:13–17

Meeting new people used to terrify me. Born with a cleft palate that went mostly uncorrected until I reached my twenties, I had a profound speech impediment. Pronouncing "s" and "j" correctly was physically impossible for me.

Just think a minute about all the words with "s" in their spelling. You can see how disruptive my handicap was to my ability to communicate. Now remember that my name is Jake. Imagine introducing yourself knowing that most listeners will misunderstand what you say.

For instance, a new football coach in middle school got to know his players by asking us our name, writing our name on a piece of masking tape, and plastering the strip of tape on our helmet. My helmet announced "Gay" to all my coaches and the rest of my team for weeks. That's what he had heard me say

111

when trying to say my name. Depending on where you grow up, that might not be a big deal today, and it really shouldn't be. But back then, for a bunch of middle school boys, it was like blood in the water of a shark tank.

Seeing how hard it was for me to make new friends and to enter into new situations, some of my family and friends gave me what they thought was helpful advice. "Just be yourself." For most people that is probably helpful advice. But the self that God made me to be happens to ask questions like this: What does it mean to be yourself?

That should be obvious. Only a person marred by too much training in philosophy—in other words, people like me—could make such an obvious piece of advice into a complicated puzzle. Right?

Well, actually, not so much.

The story of Jesus's baptism raises precisely this question. And it suggests a paradoxical answer: Being yourself is not all about you. Let's take a closer look at Matthew's account of the baptism of Jesus and I think you'll see what I mean.

When Jesus emerges from the waters of baptism, a voice from heaven says, "This is my Son, the Beloved, with whom I am well pleased."[38] God is speaking. Not just to Jesus. But to all of us.

This public message unpacks and enlarges the private message that Joseph had received in a dream before Jesus was even born. Learning that Mary was pregnant before they had had intimate relations with each other, Joseph decides to break off the engagement quietly. Joseph changes his plans when, in a dream, God tells him that Mary is a virgin and that Jesus has been supernaturally conceived by the Holy Spirit.

To speak figuratively, Joseph (and Matthew's readers) learns in that dream that Jesus has God's own DNA. But there is much more to being father and son than shared genetic makeup. God wants us to see that Jesus is more than an accidental

---

38 Matthew 3:17.

offspring. After all, we know that men can be merely biological fathers. Even if they dwell in the same house, some fathers are so absorbed in their own pursuits that they have built no substantive relationship with their sons and daughters. Still others deny, abandon, or even reject their children.

God tells the world, "I love this man. Who I am is forever bound up with who he is. And no matter what, I'm really good with that."

In other words, even for God, being himself is not all about him.

That voice from heaven tells us to look at the relationship between the Father and the Son. It defines them both at the very core. The Son can be the Son only by having a Father, and the Father can be the Father only by having a Son.

I recall lying in bed with my oldest when he was just a baby. At that instant, I realized that my life had forever changed. Andrew was not just my biological offspring. Without quite realizing it, I had given him my heart. My joy and sadness, security and fear were forever bound up with his life. My heart had laid claim to him in a way deeper than biology and more profound than any legal commitments.

This is a pale analogy—my love is sometimes misguided and more often than I like to admit mixed with fear, self-interest, or my control needs—but it illustrates to some degree what that voice was saying. God's relationship with Jesus makes God God. The Holy One is all in.

Relationships run in more than one direction. God the Father loves Jesus with a fierce, tender, unrelenting vulnerability. God initiates the relationship. Jesus returns that love as a Son. That's what he's getting at in his response to John the Baptist's reluctance to baptize him. Jesus says, "It is proper for us in this way to fulfill all righteousness."[39] He is perfectly obedient.

That word "obedient" is something of a turnoff for most of us. That's because many of us don't really get it, not in its truest

---

39 Matthew 3:15.

sense. We think about authority figures barking commands and subordinates carrying out those orders. In the postmodern West it is difficult to hear the word "obey" without filtering it through notions like power differential, submission, and coercion. But I ask you to give it a try.

Jesus hears, really hears, God's "I love you." It's not just his ears at work. God's love resonates in Jesus's marrow. Jesus surrenders himself to the one who already loves him precisely in order to be himself. To be the Beloved.

When we think about being ourselves, we tend to think in terms of self-expression and differentiation. That is to say, we think of the self as something deep within. We often hide that interior self and will be happy if and only if we bring it out, if we express it.

Correlatively, we contrast being yourself with living up to others' expectations. Many of us remain under the impression that only by differentiating ourselves from what the Existentialists called "The Herd" or the "They" can we become our authentic selves.

So, when we hear that Jesus obeyed the Father, we have to struggle to set this pattern of thinking aside. Jesus is not giving up his true self in order to please God. It is in relationship with the Father that the Son can be a Son at all. The true self is not hidden deep within. It is found in the relationships to which we surrender ourselves. This is true for Jesus. It's true for us.

At the River Jordan, Jesus lets John immerse him in that water to lay claim to his relationship with us. He's all in. In our glory and our shabbiness, in our tender mercies and our cold indifference, in our loyalty and our betrayal, in our belonging and our loneliness, in our laughter and our tears.

He becomes most truly himself when his life is no longer about him. And when we follow Jesus, we follow that same path.

God wants us to be ourselves, the selves he has dreamt about and longed for since before time. The self who aches when others suffer, who rejoices when others get good news. The self who measures success by the well-being of others. The self who finds no contentment while others know misery, who rises to defend the weak, and who refuses to sit idly by while others endure injustice.

God wants you to be yourself, and the key is to remember that being yourself is not all about you.

Reflection Questions

- Did you feel loved as a child? Did you feel unloved? What made you feel loved or unloved?
- Who is making you feel loved now? How do they make you feel loved?
- How are you at making others feel loved? In what ways do you love imperfectly even the ones you love the most? Are you hard on yourself about your imperfections? Are you understanding and gracious toward yourself? If so, what helps you to be so?
- How do you experience God's love for you?

22

Rehab

Read John 9:1–41

Brené Brown introduced me to the phrase "shame storm." If you're like me, you've been caught in one before. You just didn't know what to call it.

Shame storms can be triggered by all sorts of things, and they may take different forms for different people. But in essence, shame tells us that we're no good. We don't measure up.

Don't confuse shame with guilt. They're really very different. Guilt is actually helpful. When we know that we've done something wrong, we feel remorse. Our contrition leads us to change our ways and to mend fences.

Shame, by contrast, devastates and dismantles us. In the midst of a shame storm, I'm likely to say to myself, "You're an idiot." I feel like a fraud that's been found out. My only option seems to be to lock myself in solitary confinement, to hide myself from the world that surely rejects me now that I've been exposed for what I am, and to kick myself unconscious to save everybody else the trouble.

Here's an example of one of my shame storms.

I was a brand new philosophy teacher. Still working on my dissertation, I was given an intro to philosophy course to teach at Emory University. The lecture hall was filled with over-achieving, hyperintelligent young men and women. That is the profile of the Emory student. Intelligent. Driven. Well-educated. Sophisticated.

There's no question that I knew more about philosophy than any of them. And I'm not the dimmest bulb ever. But frankly, I was incredibly insecure about all sorts of things. The speech impediment I had grown up with had been surgically corrected only a couple of years earlier. Speaking in front of people still triggered my gag reflex. Growing up in a home in which English was a sketchy second language, my vocabulary was a little narrow, and I was sure that my education had big gaps in it.

Now add these factoids. I grew up in the working class, I was the first in my family to even attend college, and I was standing in front of sons and daughters of doctors, lawyers, professors, and CEOs.

I was feeling a little like that man behind the curtain in *The Wizard of Oz*, and I heard Toto sniffing around my feet.

Things were, to my relief, going pretty well. The students were engaged. They laughed at my jokes. They even seemed to like me personally. And then it happened.

I was writing on the board. I wrote the word *occurrence*. Only I misspelled it, replacing the *e* with an *a*. O-c-c-u-r-r-a-n-c-e. Mind you, I didn't know that I had misspelled it. Oh no. In fact, I had always thought that my misspelling was the correct spelling. That's what I thought until I heard a voice say, "Do you mean occurrence? That would be o-c-c-u-r-r-E-n-c-e." It was a voice I knew well. The smartest student in the class. The very one who routinely challenged me, outflanked me with a supe-rior vocabulary, and at times outpaced me intellectually.

Now if that happened today, I would chuckle, thank him for the spelling help, and not give it a second thought. But I was twenty-six, and I was overwhelmed. I barely got to the end of the class before succumbing to a hurricane-strength shame storm. I was sure that all those students saw me for the fraud that I was and would never respect me as their teacher again. I spent the rest of the day in a funk repeating versions of "Stupid, stupid, stupid," in my head.

Here's the difference between that young, inexperienced teacher and the man that I am today. That young Jake was convinced that his worth was bound up with his achievements. I was always trying to measure up to validate my own existence. Falling short of the mark meant that I was less lovable. Maybe not lovable at all. I was striving to fit in with all the other people who had made it, had measured up, had proved that they belonged in the lovable group.

This older Jake is still susceptible to shame storms, but those storms are neither so frequent nor so intense. And I've learned how to weather them so that I come out on the other side not only intact, but more vital and robust, more accepting of my imperfect self and, crucially, more accepting of others as just the imperfect gifts I need.

Shame no longer plays the role it once did in my life because Jesus has shown me something about him and something about me. Jesus has not come to condemn me because I haven't gotten life right. He has come to heal me, to give me a new life that I can't make for myself.

This is one of the lessons of the story of Jesus's healing of the blind man in John's Gospel.[40] The disciples asked Jesus why the man was born blind. Did he sin or did his parents sin?

They were expressing a theology of suffering common in their day. You might call it the blame the victim theology. If something rotten happens in your life, you've got it coming. It's

---

40 John 9:1–41.

a punishment for your sins. Conversely, that theology suggests that health and wealth are a reward for playing ball with God.

In this theology, God merely upholds the divine standards. God rewards those who measure up and punishes those who fall short. Moral achievement wins God's approval. Wailing and gnashing teeth in the outer darkness await moral underachievers. This is just the sort of theology that creates shame storms.

Jesus is abundantly clear. This is not how God rolls.

God goes looking for the blind (and the lame, the leprous, the sketchy, the cranky, the self-absorbed, and the clueless), not to scold them or to condemn them or even to condescend to them. God seeks out the blind to give them sight. God is a healer, not a moral scorekeeper.

The Holy One is not looking to start a club for the morally elite. In Jesus, God has opened a rehab center. The only criterion for admission is that you're sick and you really want to be made well.

You can stay as long as you admit a basic truth. In this life, you're never going to be completely recovered. At no point will you be able to look down your nose at any fellow inhabitants, nor for that matter at those who haven't stumbled in just yet. When things are going well for you, you'll say with gratitude and joy that you are recovering, but God's not finished with your rehab yet.

We are broken, and God has come to make us whole. Instead of rewarding moral performance, Jesus heals broken hearts and minds, souls and bodies.

The Pharisees will have none of this. They are the religious insiders. They know the rules like nobody else, and they follow these rules rigorously. As they see it, their rectitude gives them the status to say who is in and who is out. They are God's morality police.

There's just one problem.

If God is a healer and not a moral scorekeeper, then it's not so clear that God actually needs morality police. The Pharisees are not about to give up their status, so they refuse to accept the God that Jesus is revealing. The God of mercy and healing. Ironically, the Pharisees choose to remain blind to who God is in Jesus.

As a younger man I was blind in a way worthy of the Pharisees. I was convinced that my degrees, publications, lectures, awards, or position on the career ladder would convince the world of my worth. Would convince me of my worth. That's why I was so susceptible to shame storms. A single misstep called my entire worth into question.

I regret to say that my fear and shame about my own inadequacy prevented me from wholeheartedly affirming and accepting others in their weakness and fragility. Again and again I would try to fix people as if their lives were a problem to be solved. Or I would get frustrated and even angry when they didn't measure up after all the work I had put into them.

Everything began to change for me when I saw Jesus for who he is. Instead of the God who will love me when I am moral enough or spiritual enough, Jesus is the God who loves me when I'm a mess. His love makes me enough. And being enough frees me up to love others when they're a mess.

Don't get me wrong. I'm still in spiritual rehab. I'm not perfect. But Christ is making progress in me. And I know that God is making progress in you.

Reflection Questions

- How do you respond to your own mistakes? Do you have shame storms? Talk about a time when things fell apart or you made a significant mistake. How did you respond?
- When things go wrong, do you look for someone to blame? Talk about a time when someone did something that had a negative effect on you or someone you love. How did you respond?
- What do your answers to the previous questions say about your concept of God? Are your emotional responses in line with how you think about God?

- If you have learned to be gentler and kinder with yourself and others when things go awry, what got you there? How was God involved? How were other people involved? Were there any spiritual practices that you found helpful in this process?

23

Life after Drowning

Read Mark 1:4–11

To graduate, everyone at Oxford College of Emory University had to take drown proofing. And most everyone dreaded it.

I learned to swim before I could walk. The water doesn't bother me. In fact, most everybody in my class was at least an adequate swimmer. Spending time at the pool was not the problem as such. It was the final three tests of the class that gave it such a dreadful reputation.

This course was meant to help you survive no matter what. We learned to tread water for extended periods, swim a mile fully clothed, and even make a flotation device out of our pants. All of this was tedious, but no one was shaken by it. But we all realized that this was just the buildup to the grand finale. You see, when we say drown proofing, we really mean drown proofing. So we had to learn to survive in the water even in the event of an injury to our limbs.

First, we had to jump into the pool and swim some distance with our feet tied. For me, that was a piece of cake.

At the next class session, the teacher left our feet free and tied our hands behind our back. Strictly speaking, this wouldn't be a problem at all if you didn't need to breathe. But of course, to swim any distance at all you need air. We had to learn techniques for catching a breath without the use of our arms. This was the first time when getting enough air was real work. Most of us experienced the beginning of the panic you get when it occurs to you that maybe, just maybe, you're not going to be able to breathe.

You've probably already guessed what the last test was. With both hands and feet tied, you had to jump into the pool and swim to the other side. Mercifully, you could opt out of this test. Since I already had an A, I said no thanks. We all attended that last class session just to see if anyone would actually take this test. One brave soul did, and we all cheered and clapped as he dolphin-kicked his way to the far side of the pool.

Nobody wants to drown.

That's why there is such a class and why we have lifeguards and personal flotation devices. Drowning is a terrifying way to die. Lack of oxygen triggers a desperate panic. But I think there may be something more. In drowning, we are very aware of losing our lives.

Nobody wants to drown.

That's why baptism is such a shocking sacrament. It begins with drowning.

Along with many other denominations, we Episcopalians minimize the shock of baptism. We sprinkle baptismal candidates instead of fully immersing them. And while I fully agree with our way of doing things, I also recognize that the subtlety of our symbols requires a little explanatory help from time to time.

Baptism sets the pattern for the whole of the Christian life. Life in Jesus Christ is the way of dying and rising. In the waters of Holy Baptism we die to a narrower life in order to rise to a greater life. Every day.

For some who come to faith later in life and undergo Holy Baptism as an adult, the pattern of dying and rising may initially take the shape of dying to a life of sin and rising to a life of moral integrity. They are going through a process of cleaning up their act, and for them baptism feels like a spiritual bath.

That is their experience at the time. But as they mature spiritually, they continue to follow the same pattern of dying and rising, and the contours of the pattern no longer resemble the words of the much loved hymn: "I once was lost but now I'm found."[41] Dying and rising takes on greater depth.

We should know this already. After all, we baptize infants. Unless you have a lower view of human nature than I do, you're unlikely to say that babies are dreadful sinners before they're baptized. Something else is happening.

Mark's version of the baptism of Jesus helps us to see what that something else actually is.

Jesus was not a sinner. Like all of us, he did boneheaded things, made mistakes, and learned through trial and error. However, none of that is sin. He just had to learn how to be a human being and how to be himself. Just like the rest of us.

Okay, this is all complicated by our abiding belief that Jesus is fully human and also fully divine. The doctrine of the Trinity is the only real help here, and we just don't have time for that right now. So let's just agree to get to those questions another time and get back to Jesus's baptism.

Jesus is the very image of God. Not because he is God—but because he is human. In Genesis we learn that the Creator formed us in the divine image. So being a human and being yourself is all about growing into a richer, more winsome image of God.

For years I understood being the image of God on analogy with being a mirror. We reflect God, I thought. I now think that this mirror metaphor, though useful, can only take us so far in understanding the Christian life.

God created us not merely to reflect him, but to partake in the divine life. In John's Gospel for instance, Jesus says that he

---

41 "Amazing Grace," words by John Newton, *The Hymnal 1982* (New York: Church Pension Group, 1982), hymn 671.

abides in us as the Father abides in him.[42] Christ dwells in us. Permeates us. Infuses us with himself.

Who we are as human beings, and who we are as unique individuals, derives from our relationship with God in Christ. We become more fully the image of God as we allow God more fully to inhabit our lives. This is the greater life to which we rise when we die to artificially narrow limits that we erect in order to define what amounts to a false self.

And there's the hitch. We have to die to a self to whom we've grown accustomed—a self that we have nurtured and defended and promoted—in order to rise to greater life. And letting go of the life we've made for ourselves can be terrifying.

Any self that cannot love the Christ that it sees in the face of the other—and I mean every size, shape, orientation, social class, race, political affiliation, hygiene, dress code, and shoe size of other—is a false self. A self to which we must die if we are to rise to greater life.

Life is not about drown proofing. Preserving life at all costs. It's about letting go of the life we can make for ourselves in order to receive as a gift a life of infinite and eternal worth.

Reflection Questions

- Have you ever experienced God dwelling in you and working through you? Talk about a time that you felt like the image of God.
- Rising to greater life involves dying to narrower life. Talk about some ways of seeing yourself and seeing other people that you have died to. How has God brought you to a new, greater view of yourself and others? Share a story if you have one.
- How does your relationship with God affect your response to the death of loved ones? How about your own death?
- Do you inhabit a way of seeing the world, pursuing life, or relating to others that you are beginning to realize is narrow? Do you sense that God is offering you greater life?

---

42 John 15:1–8.

24

Wandering

Read John 1:43–51

We didn't have much of a plan. In early August of 1983, my wife, Joy, and I stepped off the plane in Frankfurt, strapped on our backpacks, and started wandering around Germany.

Less than four months earlier we had gotten married in Atlanta. Before tying the knot, we had known each other for less than a year. We were drawn together by the stuff that makes coyotes howl and mockingbirds sing.

Joy fascinated me, thrilled me, made me laugh, and occasionally utterly confused me. All in the same moment I wanted to embrace her, joke with her, stare at her, and sing with her. When I was away from her I couldn't get her off my mind. When we were together, hours sped by like minutes.

In late September we would begin studying at the Ruhr University in Bochum. Until then, we wandered from place to place, hopping trains or boats, or hiking hilly trails to places suggested by our guide book or by people we met along the way.

For a while at least we were not straining to reach a well-defined destination. And yet, our travels were far from aimless. Our wandering was drawing us closer to each other. Our journey was measured more in time together and the bond we were forming than in miles covered and places visited. During that month, and for the rest of that academic year, Joy and I came to know each other more intimately and to know the new selves that we were becoming by walking along together.

That's the nature of wandering.

Jesus wants us to wander with him. To roam through life with him. That's hard for us to get our minds around. We spend much of our time treating our lives like a goal-driven march. Getting to our destination preoccupies us. Many of us relate to Jesus as the one who will get us to where we want to go. By contrast, Jesus offers himself to us as the one we yearn to know and the one who will help us discover who we truly are just by walking with him.

In John's Gospel Jesus calls the first disciples by saying, "Come and see." Andrew and another disciple were trailing Jesus at a little distance, sort of checking him out anonymously after John the Baptist had identified him as the Lamb of God.

Jesus saw them and asked, "What are you looking for?"

"Where are you staying?" they asked.

Jesus simply said, "Come and see."

The very next day the newly minted disciple Philip invited his friend Nathaniel to join him in following Jesus. He used Jesus's own words: Come and see.

Jesus's invitation is something like this: "Walk with me for a while. Don't worry about where we will end up. We'll discover amazing things along the way. You'll feel and see and taste how God infuses even the smallest, most ordinary moments with eternal life. You'll find depths and textures of yourself that you never guessed were there. You'll be able to appreciate the beauty and goodness of people who used to irritate, bore, offend, or even frighten you."

But, here's the hitch. When we wander with Jesus, we give up marching doggedly to some destination we've already got picked out. Jesus is not our guide to our dream of paradise. He himself is the very intersection of heaven and earth. He is our very heart's desire.

The theme of wandering with Jesus runs steadily through John's Gospel.

Jesus blows Nicodemus's mind with the idea of being reborn from above. Wandering with him is the way to spiritual rebirth. As Jesus says, "The wind blows where it chooses, and you hear the sound of it, but you do not know where it comes from or where it goes. So it is with everyone who is born of the Spirit."[43]

As Jesus draws near to the Passion, he tells the disciples that all that time walking together has made them friends. They've grown close by simply stumbling along together. They haven't completely figured Jesus out, and yet they know him and yearn to know him even better. They haven't flawlessly applied his teachings to their lives nor have they managed to follow his example perfectly. They've just spent time wandering with him and with the rest of the shabby, bedraggled bunch shuffling along with him.

John's is the Gospel that features the beloved disciple. And it's the Gospel that concludes with the risen Jesus asking Peter the same question three times: Do you love me? Wandering with Jesus is all about relationship.

We now wander with the risen Jesus. Jesus still invites everyone to come and see. Only now he issues that invitation through you and me. God draws people into relationship when we invite strangers to become friends. To wander with us. All we need to say is, "Come and see."

Many of our efforts at evangelism fall flat. Frequently those efforts don't actually get started. We mistakenly assume that issuing an invitation to follow Jesus means convincing people

---

43 John 3:8.

to accept our list of concepts about God and demand an adherence to our moral code.

Think a minute about how you respond to other people. Are you drawn to people who tell you that you have to think the way they do or revise your behavior to resemble theirs? Maybe you are. But as for me, I just move on to avoid getting irritated. Instead of demanding theological conformity and moral compliance, Jesus forms relationships. Come and see, he says. Come along. Let's see where this will lead.

Sharing our relationship with Christ is not about forcing theological concepts down somebody's throat or scolding them about their moral failings. It's an invitation to walk together. To be and to do the Gospel together.

Invite others to come and see as you visit the sick, the lonely, and the imprisoned together. To join you in feeding the hungry, sheltering the homeless, providing access to medical care. Ask questions. Listen carefully. Speak sparingly. Share your time and give your presence. Tell your story with all its embarrassing twists and false starts, not to instruct, but to make yourself vulnerable and approachable.

In our own way, Joy and I are still wandering. We know each other well but there is much more to learn. We still surprise and delight each other every day. There's no telling what tomorrow will bring, but we will step into tomorrow together. That's what it means to be faithful to each other.

Similarly, we are most faithful to Jesus when we remember that we are still wandering with him. We have not arrived. There's still much for us to learn. There's no telling what tomorrow may bring. But we can trust that he will step into tomorrow with us.

Reflection Questions

- How do you see your life? Is it a linear progression, or is it filled with unexpected turns and surprise destinations? How do you respond to the idea that life is about wandering with Jesus?

- Think about one of your deepest, most abiding friendships. Talk about how your friendship has deepened over time. What are some things that you have gone through together? How has your friend helped you become yourself?
- Do you believe that Jesus calls you friend? What do you think he means by that? How does his friendship shape your daily life, your values, your self-perception, and your view of others?

Scripture Index